How to Kill a Narcissist

An ultimate guide to recovery from emotional and narcissistic abuse. Understanding and managing narcissism. How to become the narcissist's nightmare and kill a narcissist

Melody Romig

© Text Copyright 2019 (Melody Romig)
All rights reserved.

No part of this guide may be reproduced in any form without permission in writing from the publisher except in the case of brief quotations embodied in critical articles or reviews.

Legal & Disclaimer

The information contained in this book and its contents is not designed to replace or take the place of any form of medical or professional advice; and is not meant to replace the need for independent medical, financial, legal or other professional advice or services, as may be required. The content and information in this book has been provided for educational and entertainment purposes only.

The content and information contained in this book has been compiled from sources deemed reliable, and it is accurate to the best of the Author's knowledge, information and belief. However, the Author cannot guarantee its accuracy and validity and cannot be held liable for any errors and/or omissions. Further, changes are periodically made to this book as and when needed. Where appropriate and/or necessary, you must consult a professional (including but not limited to your doctor, attorney, financial advisor or such other professional advisor) before using any of the suggested remedies, techniques, or information in this book. Upon using the contents and information contained in this book, you agree to hold harmless the Author from and against any damages, costs, and expenses, including any legal fees potentially resulting from the application of any of the information provided by this book. This disclaimer applies to any loss, damages or injury caused by the use and application, whether directly or indirectly, of any advice or information presented, whether for breach of contract, tort, negligence, personal injury, criminal intent, or under any other cause of action. You agree to accept all risks of using the information presented inside this book.

You agree that by continuing to read this book, where appropriate and/or necessary, you shall consult a professional (including but not limited to your doctor, attorney, or financial advisor or such other advisor as needed) before using any of the suggested remedies, techniques, or information in this book.

Table of Contents

INTRODUCTION 7

CHAPTER 1 12

THE DISCOMFORT OF NARCISSISM 12

   1.1 WHAT IS NARCISSISM? 12
   1.2 HOW TO RECOGNIZE A NARCISSIST? 18
   1.3 VICTIMS OF NARCISSIST 24

CHAPTER 2 33

UNDERSTANDING NARCISSISTIC PERSONALITY 33

   2.1 PATHOLOGICAL NARCISSISM ... WHAT IT MEANS 33
   2.2 THE ILLUSION OF THE NARCISSIST 34
   2.3 NARCISSISM AND SELF-ANALYSIS (OR ANALYSIS OF THE SELF) CHOOSE THE CORRECT TERM 52
   2.4 THE SUFFERING BEHIND THE NARCISSISTIC MASK 56

CHAPTER 3 59

HOW TO TREAT A NARCISSIST 59

   3.1 MANAGE A NARCISSIST 59
   3.2 HOW DO YOU KNOW YOU ARE DEALING WITH A NARCISSIST 73
   3.3 CAN NARCISSISTS CHANGE? 85

3.4 How not to be overwhelmed by a narcissist 92

CHAPTER 4 98

DEFEND YOURSELF AGAINST NARCISSISTS 98

4.1 What are the causes of Narcissistic Personality Disorder? 98
4.2 How dangerous can a narcissist become? 106
4.3 10 tips to defend yourself from narcissists (Details on tips in message below) 108

CHAPTER 5 115

IN A RELATIONSHIP WITH A NARCISSIST 115

5.1 The phases of relationships with narcissists 115
5.2 Can two narcissists be in a relationship? 117
5.3 In love with a narcissist? Best ways to make it work… 118

CHAPTER 6: 123

WHAT IS THE QUICKEST WAY TO GET OUT OF A NARCISSISTIC RELATIONSHIP 123

6.1 Ask for help 123
6.2 No contact 127
6.3 Is it always right to leave a narcissist? 128

6.4 How to deal with a complicated
RELATIONSHIP WHEN CHILDREN ARE INVOLVED ..134

CONCLUSION 138

INTRODUCTION

Have you ever met a person who wants to get attention all the time but doesn't reciprocate the same? I guess you have. Such kind of people are many out there and they perceive themselves to be better than others and therefore should be treated differently. These people can insult others anyhow and they feel no empathy for you if you are hurt. In some situations, you find people who always want things done in their ways. They will claim that the approach of their doing is perfect, and your methods are a failure. Such people are egocentric and cannot accept any own error.

They, therefore, justify their incorrectness. Dealing with such people is sometimes hectic, and as a result, it has led to many broken marriages. If you have met a person with such traits, you met a narcissist. Dealing with a narcissist is hard work because, at first glance, you would believe them to be the kindest people that walk the earth. This is what they want you to think, how they draw you into their web and under their control.

Dealing with a person who suffers from narcissistic personality disorder will be difficult but this book aims to give you a heads up and a foothold in your journey.

Everyone is narcissistic to a certain level. This is because it is a normal thing to respect and love yourself without regarding other people. If not for this aspect of narcissism, the current population will have never evolved into the modern society it is today.

The narcissist displays extreme levels of self-centeredness that distort their idea of self-love. This makes them deviate from their normal functioning. The narcissist rarely contributes to society and usually exhibits anti-social behavior towards other people.

The person that suffers from narcissism doesn't have any empathy towards other people. Because of her self-regard, she doesn't recognize any actions that she makes can be unacceptable in society. She doesn't get ashamed at all, regardless of the situation.

The cause of this disorder is not exactly known. However, research has shown that one's environment could increase the chances of narcissism. Children who are excessively pampered or excessively criticized have higher chances of developing this disorder. How could this be the case while the two are on extreme ends of the spectrum?

Let's start with kids who are pampered. They grow up accustomed to getting what they want. Their parents give in to every little one of their whims. And they expect the same from life. They walk around with a sense of entitlement, wanting people to treat them the same way their parents did. Life shows them a different reality. They're in denial. They can't understand why they're not getting what they want.

They begin to live in a fantasy world, picturing themselves as successful and powerful. They feel important, even when they have not achieved much. They manipulate those around them to sing their praises. They come across as arrogant as they always want to be in control since that's what they're used to from a young age.

On the other hand, there are those people that were criticized excessively when growing up. They were made to feel as if they were not good enough. They grow up wanting to prove a point to the world, and to themselves, that they're not what their parents said of them. That's the reason they want to display every achievement and get you talking about it. They demand admiration and praise to fill that gap that was created in their childhood.

They create a fantasy about success to escape from their bruised self-esteem. They're also envious of those who have what they would wish to have. If you're a parent reading this, that right there is a pointer of how not to raise your children.

There could also be a genetic factor in this disorder. If you have members of the family with the conditions, the chances are that some of their descendants will inherit it.

A narcissistic personality disorder affects more men than women. The symptoms begin to show during teenage or early adulthood.

Can children be narcissistic? Experts suggest that although children could display similar traits such as self-centeredness and excess need for attention, they should not be labeled as such. Chances are they're just dealing with normal children's emotions.

The way you take care of your child right from birth is what makes them a narcissist. When you teach them that the world owes them something, then that is the way they will take up the world. If you tell them that they are the ones to make things work for them, then that is the way they will behave.

Everyone has a raging narcissist that they have to deal with in their lives, in one way or the other. This can be at your job, in your home or even in your love life. So, how did the person get to this point?

Are narcissistic people aware that they suffer from the condition? Well, as much as others point it out to them constantly, they refuse to acknowledge that anything is wrong with them. They get angry and defensive when anyone suggests that they should get help.

They say that if you cannot change the problem; you can change how you perceive the problem.

Many people out there are stuck in abusive narcissist relationships. It does not matter the type of abuse; be it a child-parent relationship or an adult-adult. This type of abuse brings about emotional damage. From recent studies conducted, it is believed that when a person is exposed to narcissistic abuse for a longer-term, it causes adverse physical damage to the brain.

This book is for you who wants to know more about narcissism and how deal with a narcissist person. In the book, you will discover what narcissism is and how it can be handled. You will discover how to spot a narcissist and how to deal with them, how to talk to them, how to leave them and many more things about narcissism.

Enjoy reading!

Chapter 1

The discomfort of narcissism

1.1 What is narcissism?

Who is a Narcissist?

A true narcissist is someone who suffers from Narcissistic Personality Disorder (NPD) and is a person who has an extreme interest in themselves, an inflated sense of self-importance, and someone who struggles to maintain relationships and friendships with other people. It's likely that a narcissistic will not have long-lasting friendships in their life, e.g. they won't have someone in their life who they've been friends with since childhood, whereas many other people will have at least one.

The reason for this is that narcissists push people away with their behaviour, although they don't actually mean to do it. You see, narcissists aren't trying to hurt people intentionally, they simply do it through their actions, and don't see anything wrong with what they are doing. A narcissist is never wrong in a narcissist's eyes. A narcissist's opinion is not an opinion, it is fact - that is how they see it.

How the narcissist controls you

All narcissists crave control no matter where they fall on the spectrum. And whatever control method they decide to use depends on the type of narcissist they are.

But the worse of all is the control method that makes the victim question their own sanity.

Other passive-aggressive methods include dominating stances and body languages that communicate displeasure. Narcissists may try to stand over you and give you a very deep cold stare. What many people don't get over is the need to get closure.

They want to know why the narcissist is giving them the silent treatment, they don't know what they are doing wrong and want answers. The truth is, it's the narcissist's nature to use invalidation and withdrawal to nourish his grandiosity.

Usually, it has very little to do with your actions and no matter how much you try to find closure, you will most likely not get it.
The narcissist will never be satisfied with your effort, no matter how hard you try to prove your loyalty. You will be compared with someone else and the narcissist will withhold the acknowledgment of all the help you have

rendered in times past.

In the end, it will make you feel that you are not quite good enough. Playing the victim is a very effective method of control.

Mockery, public humiliation, and criticism are tools that the narcissist uses to establish control.

A snide remark here about your appearance, a comment there about how silly you are, which all appear to be indirect are tools the narcissist uses for his own personal gain.

They may say things like, "oh it was just a joke", "Oh, don't be sentimental", "you are overreacting", or "It's just for your own good, the truth is bitter" in front of an audience so they appear respectable and if the audience laughs, the narcissist feels a boost of power by seeing your discomfort.

Narcissists get their ego boost from tormenting, taunting, and punishing whoever is their chosen target. They gain control by getting an emotional reaction. They will create dramas and makeup stories. They may recreate history just to provoke an emotional reaction to trigger a supply of your energy. They look for your exposed emotional buttons in a manner of speaking so they can press them for fun and entertainment. They assure themselves of how easily they can control you. Therefore, your reactions validate the narcissist's power dominance and how important they are.

A narcissist will also want to control your level of self-confidence and self-worth. If you speak up for yourself in situations like this, they will project their aggression on to you by saying that you are aggressive when you are just trying to be assertive and get your message across. So, the narcissist will establish control using power struggles, games, and other subtle methods.

The narcissist is also good at using fear as an instrument of torture. They will use warnings, forecasts, and predicting how bad things are and how terrible they were and how your actions will only cause you pain in the long run. The reason is simple.

If you are fearful, you are more easily manipulated and are more likely to believe their horrific predictions and when this is shared with paranoia, it bonds you together.
Therefore, if you can see them as your only source of wisdom, hope, and security, that gives them control over you.

Seeds of doubt will be planted, and the narcissist will watch you question your own sanity because if their doubts can influence your decision, then this proves how powerful they are in your life.

They will intimidate you into making a choice that suits them. They will do whatever it takes to sabotage your success because this is evidence of their power over you and they want you to turn only to them and see them as an authority on everything in your life. The more dependent you are on them, the more they are able to control you.

Having an emotional reaction to the apprehensive rage of the narcissist opens you up to their control since your emotions are a key thing they prey on. Your reactions demonstrate their superiority and affirm your inferiority. Therefore, be mindful of your emotional reactions.

Learn discernment and how to manage your emotional state. This may take some practice, but it can be done and it's a worth skill to master that will benefit all areas of your life.

Some narcissists thrive on secrecy, they will intentionally confuse you by implying that privacy and secrecy are one and same. But they are not. Secrecy is used to hide something whereas privacy is used to protect something.

The narcissist might imply they are protecting you from something for your own good when in fact they are hiding something that would devastate the illusion they have created.

It could be addictions, history of abuse and violence, financial status, issues with the law, marital status... basically anything. They will also use secrecy to remain mysterious and invasive which can be alluring to the unsuspecting person, but they are capable of anything, even if it means your never finding out the truth.

Secrecy is what a narcissist uses to preserve its control dynamic. Secrecy involves turning a blind eye to wrongdoing. It is not unusual for a narcissist to tell its victims to prove their loyalty by turning a blind eye to abuse or some kind of injustice that is being perpetrated. Since a narcissist lacks empathy, you are going to be saddled with the burden of participating in some kind of wrongdoing every time you prove your loyalty to them by keeping their secrets. It is important to note that secrecy is not a component of any healthy relationship.

Narcissists will also expect you to keep their rage episodes a secret, so they terrorize you into a state of secrecy even if you so much as utter a word to another party. Therefore, if the narcissist expects you to keep a secret, they are expecting you to participate in a lie and their game of manipulation.

Gaslighting

Gaslighting can be said to be a form of psychological manipulation where the perpetrator tries to sow seeds of doubt in an individual that they have targeted. The aim is to make their target question their memory, perception, and sanity.

Narcissists attempt to psychologically destabilize the victim and seek to invalidate the legitimacy of the victim's experience of their own reality. It is a form of psychological bullying.

1.2 How to recognize a narcissist?

A sense of entitlement and pre-eminence

Because of their overestimated sense of importance, narcissists expect favourable treatment whenever they go. They consider themselves special and believe that they should get everything they want.

They expect everyone around them to be at their beck and call and comply with their every wish and whim. If you don't comply and meet their every need, then they term you as useless.

Meticulousness

Many narcissists have an extremely high sense of perfection. They believe that things should happen exactly as planned, and life should be as they envision it in their minds. This is an impossible demand in the real world, which results in the narcissist feeling miserable and depressed all the time.

Narcissists who are inclined to perfection are very difficult to please. Nothing you do will be right enough, and you are always to meet their infinite needs for admiration, love, service, or purchases. Failure to meet these desires may lead to dismissal. They cannot take a "no" and often expect others to inconvenience themselves so that they can serve them.

They want to be in control

We have established that most narcissists are perfectionists, and when they feel things are not working out to their stands, they develop this great need to controlling other words. They will do anything possible to be control of a situation and manipulate it to their liking.

With their unreasonably high sense of entitlement, they will demand to control events because they believe it is the logical thing to do. In essence, they have everything figured out in their minds.

They have a storyline in mind and have assigned specific roles to each person in that particular set up. If any person behaves contrary, the narcissist becomes very agitated because you have unsettled what was in the script. You are a threat to their desired outcome. What they see in you is a mere character in their internal play, not a human being who has his own thoughts and feelings.

Thrive in the blame game

While the narcissist would desire to be in control, they never want to be responsible for an undesirable outcome. When things go contrary to their plans or desired outcome, the narcissist will place all the responsibility and blame on other people. It cannot be their fault but someone else.

They may generalize the blame all' teachers are the same, all policemen are corrupt, etc. all they may direct the blame to a particular person or system- father, sibling, the laws of the land, etc. In most cases, the narcissist will blame the one person who is the most loyal and emotionally attached to them.

This dedicated admirer is the safest to blame because the chances of denying or rejecting the blame are very minimal. The narcissist has to maintain the cover-up of perfection, and this can only be achieved by constantly putting the blame on someone or something else.

Thrill-seekers

Narcissists are adrenaline addicts who sprawl from their deeply rooted desire to be praised and get positive attention. They will describe the overwhelming situation in depth or in a bid to gain solicited admiration from those around them.

If you should dare to confront them for the dangers they are exposing themselves to by being adrenaline junkies, they will quickly dismiss you off. They will try to show you how everyone else around them is useless, and that is why they engage in risky activities to try and save the day.

Anyone working with a narcissist will find themselves in a roller coaster, swinging in random directions. You will conform to the activity that brings the maximum thrill to the narcissist. When the adrenaline rush hits, strategic plans are thrown out of the window and replaced by reactivity to a self-inflicted crisis. The bottom line is that narcissist is forever chasing thrill because the resulting excitement makes them feel good about themselves.

The excitement also serves as an outlet for all the pressure and aggression that is normally bottled up in them.

Extreme sensitivity to criticism

Narcissists believe that they must be seen as faultless, superior, or infallible. There are either perfect or worthless. To them, a middle ground does not exist. They can't tolerate the least form of criticism because they live in a world of fantasy where no wrongdoings exist.

Therefore no matter how calmly you suggest for ways that they can employ to change their unwelcome behaviour, they will react defensively or withdraw altogether. They will say anything in an effort to justify their behaviour, and they will expect you to understand and move on with life as normal.

They will attack and hurl all manner of insults to their critics and banish them from their perceived glorious presence. Narcissists will expect their opponents to be devastated when not in their coverage, and this gives them a sense of pride and importance. Surprisingly, the same people who dread to be criticized are overly critical of other people. They can see their own problems but believe other people are problematic and need to change.

Lack of a sense of humor

Narcissists are too serious for life. They don't get jokes, and they don't make jokes except for a few sarcastic remarks and weird puns. Their lack of empathy makes them not to grasp the context and emotional aspects of the words, actions, jokes, and humor expressed. For a person to laugh at a joke or make a humorous relevant he/she must, first of all, understand the context and effect of the people around him. Narcissists lack this important concept and consequently specialize in sarcasm, which they mistake for wits.

Have undefined interpersonal boundaries

Narcissists will unconsciously view others as extensions of themselves. They can't really tell where they end and where the other person begins.

They regard other people as existing solely to serve them and will disregard their needs, family obligations, and any other duty that their loyal followers have to fulfil. They are regarded as 'narcissists supply,' existing mainly to cater to their personal needs, and therefore it is difficult for the narcissist to think of them indecently. They generally expect their devotees to be at their beck and call.

The porous boundaries are what will

make such people to inappropriately dominate conversations and even disclose intimate details about their lives. They are likely to share embarrassing things they have done or said without considering how others might react to such words.

They will most likely brag about things or blurt out words that others may find distasteful, demeaning, and overall offensive.

1.3 Victims of narcissist

The victims of narcissistic abuse frequently share similar traits that mark them as easy to manipulate. While this may be unconscious on the part of the narcissist, they are attracted to a handful of traits that are the most conducive to the narcissist getting what he wants. When you understand what the narcissist values most in a target, you then learn how to guard yourself and not fall victim due to your own personality.

Codependent

Codependency is a sign of a dysfunctional relationship. Though it is often used to refer to people around a drug addict that enable the continued addiction, it is also relevant in relation to the narcissist. The codependent does not acknowledge that there are any problems in her relationship. She decides to disregard or ignore her own emotions and needs because focusing on herself has never been conducive to her relationship or having a good time. She has learned that walking on eggshells, catering to every whim of the other person keeps the other person happy, which in turn means she is safe.

She lives in denial in order to survive and oftentimes completely detaches herself from situations around her in order to survive. She goes through the motions without really feeling.

She walks through life and her relationship as a husk of a person, pouring every bit of herself into bettering the other person. The narcissist loves the codependent because the codependent will absolutely put time into pleasing the narcissist. Her own feeling of self-worth is entirely related to caring for others, to a fault. There is a fine line between compassionate and codependent, and the codependent has taken her kindness to the extreme of martyring herself out for the narcissist's own benefit. Her intentions are kind, but the mark is missed. The narcissist is simply enabled in his behaviors, believing that they are justified. This creates a destructive environment for the codependent that the narcissist thrives within. Ultimately, the narcissist feels that the codependent is the ultimate target. The codependent already has low self-esteem, attempts to do things with good intentions, and has the intense desire to help those around her. The narcissist does not hesitate to take advantage of this person, knowing that he will more easily get what he craves, and the codependent never leaves because she sees no reason to.

Caregiver Personality

Similar to the codependent, but less extreme, the caregiver personality type is quite attractive to the narcissist. While this person may not necessarily have low self-esteem, he does have good intentions and the desire to care for another individual. The caregiver naturally wants to help other people.

He sees everyone as deserving of love and help and would give the shirt off of his back to someone if it would better the other person's experience. The caregiver is selfless and dedicated to bettering the lives of those around him. He is patient and willing to put up with far more abuse or mistreatment than the average person because he believes that the other person deserves to be cared for. The compassionate, patient nature of the caregiver is exactly what the narcissist needs.

She will believe that this person will be willing to put in the effort to ensure that the narcissist is cared for and that with some manipulation and effort on the narcissist's part, has the potential to be browbeaten into codependency. The narcissist craves someone who is dedicated to caring for her, and the caregiver is quite likely to do so.

Empathetic

Good targets for the narcissist are empathetic. Like the caregiver and codependent, those who are quite empathetic typically enjoy taking care of other people to ease their pain.

The empath can feel the pain of other people so intimately it is as if she is the one being exposed to the cause of the pain herself and she seeks to alleviate that pain in others.

She does not want those around her to suffer in any way and will do whatever she can to help. The narcissist knows this and knows that empaths are particularly in tune with their feelings.

The narcissist can weaponize her empathy and use it against her, playing on guilt to keep her in line. He knows that the empath will be easy to manipulate simply because she is so susceptible to guilt trips. Empathy, being one of her best traits as an individual, becomes her weakness and the narcissist takes advantage of it in order to better himself.

Has What the Narcissist Wants

This may be one of the only times the narcissist will pick out a target that is not easily manipulated or controlled. She may see someone else with what she wants and choose to befriend them in order to learn their secrets or have some of the benefits of their power.

She will likely mirror this person quite closely, mimicking their actions in order to learn from them. If she is able to get close to the person who has what she wants, she may be able to get some by default.

For example, imagine a narcissist who has befriended the mayor of a town. Any time she goes out with the mayor, she gets treated with similar levels of prestige simply because she is in the company of the mayor, and over time, her knowing the mayor may even raise her own prestige in town.

If people know she is close to the mayor, they may treat her better in hopes of her good word getting back to him, and she preys on this. She can use this to her advantage, and over time, she is eventually recognized in her small community as well and she has done nothing but draw the mayor into believing they are friends.

Dysfunctional or Abusive Upbringing

Those who have grown up in dysfunctional or in abusive environments often never learned what healthy or normal truly looks like in regards to relationships.

They never learned how to identify when something is dangerous, abnormal, or worth avoiding. All of the abuse and dysfunction became the individual's normal, which means his or her tolerance for putting up with a narcissist's abusive, manipulative antics may be far beyond what it should be.

The narcissist knows this and seeks to use it to his advantage. He knows that the one who grew up abused is not likely to understand what healthy relationships look like, and therefore, she will never understand what it is she is missing.

She will assume whatever was modelled for her during childhood is normal and what should be expected, thinking that there is nothing better beyond that.

For example, imagine you grew up with parents who hated each other's guts but could not afford to divorce while still sustaining the children. You grew up watching your parents argue and hate each other, disrespecting each other at every opportunity, and calling each other names regularly.

Though you may know that your parents' relationship was not happy, you may struggle to dissociate that association with healthy relationships. You understand that they were not happy but you are almost destined to repeat those mistakes in your own relationships, and would not think twice about a partner that may behave similarly.

To you, they are not as alarming and foreign as they would be to someone who grew up with parents who doted on each other. The narcissist will take that tolerance and push it to the extreme, knowing it can only benefit him and his desires.

Nonconfrontational

Those who fear or avoid confrontation simply want to live a life free of conflict. They are typically quite easy-going and the narcissist sees this easy-going nature and desire to live without fighting and decides to take advantage of it.

The narcissist's manipulation tactics require her to not be called out when she attempts to control a situation and those who hate conflict or confrontation are the most likely to avoid calling out the narcissist's antics.

The nonconfrontational are far more likely to decide to give in to the narcissist's demands and suffer in silence than actually cause an issue, knowing that calling out the behaviours would result in exactly what the narcissist wants to avoid.

It becomes a situation in which the nonconfrontational person has to decide between being miserable and not calling out the abuse or being miserable after calling out the abuse and inviting more of it. The narcissist understands this tendency to avoid conflict and seeks out people who will not fight back.

He takes advantage of the person who avoids confrontation simply because it betters his situation.

Low Self-Esteem and Lack of Confidence

Both low self-esteem and low confidence lead to someone who is easily manipulated, as both of these people crave love, but feel as though they are unworthy or undeserving of it.

They feel as though they are impossible to love, seeing their flaws as their entire identity as opposed to just a small part of who they are.

The narcissist knows this; the narcissist oftentimes seeks to break down other people's self-esteem solely because those with lower self-esteem are easier to manipulate.

If at all possible, the narcissist will go for someone with low self-esteem solely because she wants to get what she wants with the least amount of effort.

The path of least resistance in this instance is the path that leads to someone who already has low self-esteem or low confidence.

If the person the narcissist has targeted already feels badly about himself, he will be that much easier to manipulate. The work is already half-finished, and all the narcissist will have to do is add the finishing touches to groom the individual into whatever she wants.

Chapter 2

Understanding narcissistic personality

2.1 Pathological narcissism ... what it means

Someone with pathological narcissist disorder usually has a one-sided sense of ability or importance. They have impressive thoughts about their social value as compared to other people. They think they should be more admired, treated, praised and that they are more valuable than others. These are the aspects that are brought about by the distortion of the brain as a result of the disorder.

They include:

- A heightened sense of self-importance
- A deep need for attention

- Lack of empathy
- Envy
- Inflated sense of entitlement
- Great fantasies of success
- Need for control
- Fragile self-esteem

2.2 The illusion of the narcissist

Now, let's analyze what goes on in the mind of a narcissist.

I am the best

One prominent behavior of your pathological narcissist is a bloated sense of self; the big ego, the idea that everything and everyone should revolve around them. Because of this, the narcissist will feel entitled to privileges and have very poor boundaries when it comes to relating to others.

This person will most likely have very little regard for etiquette or protocols. They will expect you to treat them special and will want you to see them, notice them, and even worship them for their achievement.

A pathological narcissist may also exhibit arrogance, which is often nothing more than deep-seated fear.

I can't be wrong

A narcissist is not easily influenced by day-to-day experiences like you and me.

Experiences in daily life come with ups and downs and these often help us in our daily lives to become more mature emotionally and psychologically: we gain a more realistic view of life, how it works, and what to expect and not to expect.

But narcissists are resistant to introspection and to the thought that they could be wrong, since they have an inflated sense of self. Instead, they will project this failure onto you.

Beneath all the persona of arrogance and self-aggrandizement of the narcissist is the feeling of emptiness and the lack of introspection.

You should be like me

When relating to others, the narcissist will use the same strategy with different people. They are often very good at putting people on a pedestal. They will overvalue you and devalue just as quickly. You could be humiliated and treated in a passive-aggressive fashion and even abused. This is also why most narcissists are domestic abusers.

They view people as an extension of themselves. They see people as their mirror-images. If you are smart and beautiful and shiny, they are attracted to you and will idealize you.

But as soon as you do something, they would not you do or have a contrary opinion to that which they hold, they become quickly disappointed and will often try to put you down.

They are not often able to see that people should have a view that is contrarian, or have a life, or live in a way that is different from what they consider as ideal. Devaluing others is what the narcissist is good at.

Here are some of the things that narcissists say that will help you identify them;

"After all the money I have given you."

This is aimed at making you feel guilty and then change the subject of an ongoing argument. You will ask yourself why you are asking the person so many questions when she had assisted you with some money before.

The aim of the narcissist is to try and turn the tables so that you don't see her as the bad person she is and instead forget all about what the original argument was all about.

"After all the things that I have done for you."

When the person with NPD feels as if she is losing the argument, she will change the subject to a past time when you had the need for them. For instance, if they needed a place to stay, or they needed you to help them shift an item. They will end up pointing it out even when the issue is not related to what you are talking about and push till you see their point of view.

What they aim for is that you end up apologizing for the behavior, yet you are the one that has been wronged.

"You don't have Respect for Me."

This is a very common phrase that the narcissists use to make you fall into their trap.

A person suffering from NPD thinks he or she deserves all the respect you can give them yet they don't behave the right way. If you don't follow what they tell you, or if you even look at them in a certain way, the narcissist will start arguing, and when you try to talk back at them, they will throw in the respect card.

Remember that for someone to ask for respect from you; they also need to show you that they respect you. Respect is always 2-way.

"You Never Appreciate"

It is highly likely that you always say thank you, but since the narcissist expects recognition for anything and everything they do, they will still dangle it in your face that you don't appreciate whatever they do.

You need to know that people that suffer from this disorder expect you to say thank you for everything that they do. If you thought that they do all they do for the sake of making you feel good, then you are wrong – think again.

"You Will Regret This"

This is another guilt trip that you will be taken on the whole way. Maybe you haven't said anything bad at all, but since the narcissist feels like making you feel guilty, they will try to make it look like you just made the worst mistake of your life.

Unless it is something that you have done and it is so bad that even you feel guilty yourself, you don't need to feel so guilty that you start getting worried about saying what you had to say.

Additionally, you also have a right to say something, or to do something that you see is right by you. When you do this, try and make sure that you believe in yourself so that you stand firm when you are told things that will make you feel guilty.

"You will regret it when I'm gone."

This is also something to make you feel guilty so that you feel the way the other person wants you to feel. This is usually used by a parent on s sibling to make them do something that the parent wants. If you are talking to a narcissist and they feel that they are losing the argument, they will usually feel as if you are pushing then into a corner and they will go to any length just to back out of it.

They keep on reminding you of the fact that one day they will die and you might be the cause of it, and you will have to live with the horrible things that you have done. These are also used by elder siblings on the young ones, and the aim is to upset the younger ones into submission. Now imagine saying such a statement to a ten-year-old, and then expecting the kid to be normal!

"You Can't Take a Joke."

Many times, when a narcissist insults you, and you take offense, they tend to try to downplay it so that it seems that you are exaggerating. They try to imply that whatever they said wasn't as serious as it seemed and it was just a joke. It might hurt your feelings, and you get upset, but they see it as if you cannot take a joke at all.

The truth is that it is the narcissists that cannot take a joke at all. When this happens, you need to bite your tongue and then show them that you aren't bothered at all. Remember that the narcissist is just after an argument and nothing else.

"What Will People Think?"

Most people suffering from NPD are very obsessed with the image that they portray to the public. They want their family and other people to think of them as the best people in the world when, in the real sense, they aren't.

They expect the child always to watch whatever they say to their parents so that they don't tarnish their image. Remember that the narcissist has two sides to them – the way you know them and the way everyone else knows them. On your part, you might think that the person is caring, kind, and generous and takes good care of the kids while in the real sense, they aren't the way they portray themselves.

"You Can't..."

People that suffer from NPD are very controlling. They want you to do something in such a way that they control everything. If you question them as to why you shouldn't do something the way you want to do it, they will tell you that they know what needs to be done all the time, which is wrong.

For instance, they will tell you that they expect you to do a particular task because they are the ones that gave birth to you! In truth, they just want to enforce their power on you and make you feel awkward. So, if you wish to work along with what they want, try to go for reverse psychology. Tell them you want to do something when, in reality, you wish to do something else.

"This is My House"

This is common with narcissists that wish to show you that they are in control. Well, you might be their kid, but they want to make it clear that you live in their house. They will emphasize the fact that they pay the bills and that you have no control over what you do in the house. However, you will realize that they say this to kids that are very young, even ten years old.

"It Is Jealousy"

People that suffer from NPD are very jealous. They will get jealous over anything – people who are good looking, people with more money than them, better houses, better cars and more. In turn, they will think that all people are like them when in reality most of the people don't care what happens.

They will get jealous over any achievement that you have, even that new dress that you have just bought from the local boutique.

"Did you see What She Was Wearing?"

They will try to pick fault with each and every one. They get satisfaction from making someone feel bad about themselves and will comment about anything and everything ranging from clothes to their weight.

"I feel it too."

They try to make sure that they are always far worse so that they can grab their attention each time. If you say that you are suffering from a headache, they will have a worse headache than you do. If you say that you have a stomachache, they will come up with a story of how theirs is worse than yours, just to get the attention they need from you.

"Theirs is dirtier."

The chances are likely that the narcissist will have a house that is cleaner than anyone else in the neighborhood! It can also be possible that they have a specific date for cleaning the house, just to make sure that they have a point to complain at all times.

They most probably have a specific day

just for cleaning, whereby they run the cleaning right from the top of the house to the basement, and they will make it be known to everyone that they are cleaning up.

"I don't like you that much right now."

This is the narcissist way of telling you that you have some making up that you need to do if you want to get back in their good books. This is just to force the apology from you even in times when you haven't made any mistake at all. Usually, the house gets back to normal in a few days or so, but till then, you need to make do with the tantrums.

"I love you more than you know."

When a person suffering from NPD utters these words, they are lying to you. All they want is to play with your emotions so that they mimic what you are telling them. For instance, if you tell them that you love them, they will want to make it seem like they are the ones that love you more than anyone else.

They usually say these words when they have something to hide, or they want to show you that they appreciate you when in the real sense, they don't.

"It isn't as expensive as mine."

That new thing that you just purchased,

the new painting in the sitting room or the new car that you just got won't make the narcissist any excited. Instead, it will make them even more jealous and will set off a stream of self-praise that will even end up making them talk of things that they don't have.

They will first appreciate what you have acquired; then they will go ahead to say how theirs is far much better than what you have. For instance, if you get a new dress, they will compare it to the one that they have.

"It Cost This Much"

The narcissist will always look for ways to belittle you. If you have something that you have just acquired and you wish to show them, they will ask you how much it cost for you to buy it. When you tell them the price, they will compare it to what they already own and then say how much it cost for them to own it.

Usually, the cost is more than what you will have bought your dress; however, much you will have paid for it.

The truth is that they don't wish you well; all that they mean is that you bought the dress, but it isn't as good as what they have in their wardrobe.

They are envious of anything you say that will paint you in a better light than them.

For instance, they will say how good the dress is, but they will then go ahead to tell you that the dress doesn't suit your skin tone at all.

"I just paid for your dinner."

They will always throw a situation where they feel they did something for you in your face. They will go ahead to tell others how they bought the dress for you or how they gave you most of the money that you used on the dress.

They will tell people how they were the ones that helped you start off in life when, in the real sense, they hosted you for just a few days.

The truth is that they don't do this to look kind like any parent would, but they do this because they are looking for that new argument that you are trying to avoid.

If you are wise, you will never accept any help from the narcissist because it just represents a way for them to get back at you later on. This is because they will try and use it against you at some point in the future.

"They saw me do it and are just copying me."

People that suffer from NPD can be extremely petty, and they always think that other people are always copying things off them. They will see that the new dress that that lady down the street will wear is an exact replica of what they are wearing. They must have copied them, or they followed them to the same store.

"I won't Mind."

They always try to imply that they were not invited somewhere in the first place. The truth is that they mind a lot, but they just want to show that they are better at managing their emotions compared to other people. Don't ever show them that you are busy because they will try to make it look as if they didn't want to be there in the first place. The next thing is that they will sulk for a long time and you won't even be able to see them at your door again.

"You won't be invited."

You will find a close friend or colleague, or even family member of the narcissist being alone during a major event and yet the person suffering from NPD won't bother inviting them over. They might insist that the invitation is "family only," yet you will find other people in the event that aren't part of the family.

This goes ahead to show that the narcissist has no empathy at all for other people, only themselves. They don't consider other people to be important to them.

"It isn't important."

The chances are that the narcissist is looking to argue with you again. When you try to retaliate or turn the argument around, you will be met with a saying that they don't even need the item at the moment. This is a tactic aimed at making you feel guilty or for you to apologize for something that you have not done.

"You don't have the right to speak to me like that."

Here, the narcissist wants to imply that they are special in a particular way. Usually, they have said something to you that you also retaliate on, and due to this, they want to make anything you said to seem terrible. They want to speak to you in a bad way then they expect you not to retaliate.

"Don't talk to me in that tone."

They want to project something to you. They know that they have talked to you in a wrong way, and they know that the tone of your voice has changed. They want to make it look as if the tone of your voice is so terrible that they don't want it at all. They want to make it seem worse than it already is. However, try to make sure that you dot fall for the gimmick because they want to force you to apologize over something that you haven't done.

"She is more like my sister."

Narcissists want to show that they have a special bond between them and the next person. Due to this, they want to show that the friendship they share with the person is more special compared to what you share with the person.

"Jane might be your friend, but when she needs something, she usually comes straight to me."

They want to make your special friendship seem less special than what they share.

"I can't remember."

This usually arises when you wish to show them that you know them from way back. However, narcissists never forget, though they will pretend that they have forgotten. Maybe you have asked them about something that is needed at that moment, but they start behaving as if it is a big deal.

They might not be willing to tell you what happened because when they remember, it will seem as if they are making you take precedence over what is important to them at the time.

It will be easier for them to tell you that they don't remember rather than start explaining their reactions.

"They are Not Ill"

People suffering from NPD have no sympathy for other people at all. They don't have the time for emotions, even when faced with a situation that requires them to be remorseful. For example, if they are the bosses at a certain company and someone is ill, they will always say that the person is pretending.

They will try to imply that the person that is off work is pretending. However, when they are ill, they will want to attract all the attention that they need as well as sympathy.

If you wish to be in their good books always it is important that you keep on asking them how they feel and how they are doing when they get sick; otherwise, you are in for some tongue lashing!

"It's not my fault at all."

The narcissist never admits that they are the ones at fault when a mistake happens. This happens even when you back them down into a corner. They will always have the right words to say to make you feel better. For instance, they will apologize then say something like "I'm so sorry that I hurt your feelings, but I didn't mean to make it come across that way."

The truth is that it was their fault, but since they are looking for a way out, they will not want you to react negatively, so they will make sure they get out of the loop.

"I swear..."

This type of parents will always try to make things look the way they are and will try to convince you that they didn't have any hand in something.

Truly, most normal people won't swear on the names of their family if something hadn't gone the way it was supposed to go. But since you have put them in a corner, the narcissist will try as much as they can to make you take their version of the story.

They will swear over their family's lives without any care in the world. The aim is to convince you that they are genuine when deep in their hearts they know that they have made a mistake that they need to redeem themselves from.

"You have made it up."

This is the version of them saying that you are a liar. It is usually very annoying when someone goes ahead to tell you that you are a liar when in truth, you aren't.

They expect you to spend the whole day explaining to them why you did it and how you did it so that you can satisfy their ego.

Since you don't have the luxury of spending countless hours explaining something that you didn't do, it is easier if you just accept the accusation so that life can go on.

"Stop exaggerating."

Some of the narcissists are good at making sure that you look crazier than you already are. They want to wish things in such a way that they look legit when in the real sense, you did the right thing.

They will make it seem as if you don't know what you are saying, or they want it to look as if you are exaggerating some of the things.

"I can't remember saying that"

They usually try to imply that they have no recollection whatsoever of something that happened, even if they are the ones that did it. Once you confront them, it becomes very frustrating, especially when they deny any knowledge of what happened.

Remember that they have a good memory and will remember everything that happened years ago, so the chances are that they won't remember saying anything to that effect.

They also allege that they are never wrong, and you know that this isn't true at all.

"Stop getting upset over nothing."

They don't take your emotions to mean anything. All they are looking at is that they made a snide remark then they wish you don't get upset. They will try to make a huge matter seem trivial, and yet, in reality, it isn't.

"Act your age."

They project their weaknesses to you as well. The narcissist is usually immature and will try to make you act your age so that they project whatever they are up for to you. They will make it seem like you are acting like a small child when, in reality, you are acting your age.

2.3 Narcissism and self-analysis (or analysis of the self) choose the correct term

This can be a difficult concept to grasp, but it can be life-changing once you understand it. To put it simply, you are not your thoughts.

The mind is a constant swirl of thoughts—many of which happen so quickly that you never even notice them. They can be extreme, upsetting, pleasurable, gentle, offensive, violent, or kind.

Some happen frequently, while others may have only happened once or twice in your entire life. Many have yet to be thought. Some thoughts are about things in the world, and some are about other thoughts. Some thoughts are closely tied to specific people and situations in your life, while others are more broad and general.

Despite your ever-changing thoughts, there is a part of you that has always been the same. Close your eyes. Allow yourself to connect with your breath, settling into your body and the present moment. When you feel calm and centred, think back to your six-year-old self. Try to step into that little child and see the world through his or her eyes. Notice how it feels to be that version of yourself. Some things are dramatically different.

However, some things are the same. There is a part of you that was present then, and is present now. This is what gives you a sense of unbroken continuity between the different stages of your life. This part of you is constant. It is unaffected by your thoughts.

Primarily, thoughts assign labels and solve problems. This ability works well when it's applied to problems in the outside world. It lets people figure out how to build houses, drive cars, and balance a check book. But that same label-making ability doesn't always help when applied to the self. When people label themselves, they create problems for their minds to solve.

For example, your mind may label you as weak or stupid in response to a situation. This creates the problem of how to not be weak or stupid. Things can quickly get out of hand when a person identifies with her own self-labels.

This is what is meant by the term conceptualized self. There are an infinite number of possible conceptualized selves. Each person has hundreds, thousands, or even millions of them. For example, you might have a conceptualized self that is about having been bullied in fifth grade, one about the success of graduating from college, and one about having a successful career. Much of a person's psychological distress actually comes from identifying with his own self-directed thoughts.

Suddenly, you are stupid, worthless, weak, or ugly. Rather than recognize these as labelled parts of yourself, you mistake them for your actual self.

In contrast, the part of you that has always been there, regardless of what was happening and how you felt, is the observing self.

It is the part that watches your own experience.

It defies labels because it simply watches your mind's attempts to label it. When people meditate, they are connecting with this larger self, watching their internal processes of labelling and problem solving while identifying with none of them.

Both of these parts exist in a context. They are both "you." One changes constantly with thoughts and feelings, the other is unchanging. If you pull back for an even broader perspective, you include the context in which both these parts exist as yet another aspect of self. This is called the self-as-context.

One way of thinking about these different parts of yourself is to imagine the sky. The sky is home to all sorts of activity: weather systems, clouds, birds, wind, rain, hurricanes. None of these things, on its own, is the sky. They are all parts of the sky. Even if you take them all together, they still don't add up to "the sky".

The sky is the place where these things happen. It is the context in which weather occurs, in which birds fly, and in which the sun shines. In this example, the clouds and birds are thoughts and feelings while the sky itself is the self-as-context.

As another example, imagine a forest.

Forests are teeming with life. Some of that life is pleasant to us, like flowers, deer, or babbling brooks. Other life in the forest is unpleasant to us, like mosquitoes, spiders, poison ivy, or snakes. People are like the forest. Everyone has parts to which they assign positive and negative labels, but those parts are balanced by the other objects in the forest.

Everyone is home to many different selves. There are happy selves, angry selves, ambitious selves, and frightened selves. If you make the mistake of thinking that a single conceptualized self is the whole picture, then you mistake the forest for the trees.

2.4 The suffering behind the narcissistic mask

Narcissism can be looked at as a disorder in the way that their brains don't work the same as a normal empathic individual and are highly dysfunctional. They can be viewed as wounded children in an adults body due to their belief that only there needs matter, that there is nothing wrong with them and the behaviours they display, They punish, hurt or destroy anyone they feel envious of, struggle in their ability to regulate their self-esteem and have a fragile sense of self.

The narcissist, or one with traits of narcissism, has an overestimated sense of self-importance, an exploitative mentality, and a severe craving for attention. The narcissist usually feels like he or she is smarter than everyone else and almost never admits to a fault.

Craig Malkin, the author of Rethinking Narcissism, explained that in reality, some narcissists are not all about looks, money or even fame. There are some of them that are very subtle in being narcissistic.
They do not exhibit any of the obvious signs.

So, if we aren't careful, we can easily become enmeshed, used by them or in worse cases trapped by them.
He also said that the common desire amongst all narcissists is that they have this all-consuming drive to feel special among every other person. They go about this drive in different ways.

The data that has come in from clinicians, researchers, and hospitals on the percentage of the general population with NPD is going to vary from less than one percent to 6.2 percent. However, it is common to see this more in men compared to women. Statistics show that at least 50 percent, though sometimes, as high as 75 percent, of those diagnosed with this disorder are going to be men.

The reason for this could be in the way that boys and girls will deal with criticism. Girls are more likely to take that criticism and internalize it, but boys are more likely to act out as their response to it.

One explanation for why this happens could be in the way the brand functions for girls and boys. This difference can explain, at least in part, the traditional behaviour roles of males and females as well.

If the role of the female is to nurture, it is more likely that women are going to give up their narcissism in order to tend to the needs of someone else. Because of this, the female is less likely to suffer from NPD than a man. This doesn't mean that she will never have to deal with this issue; it simply means that it is less likely.

It is possible that learned behaviour, which can be reinforced by societal expectations and more, can mean that even women may deal with this disorder as well.

Chapter 3

How to treat a narcissist

3.1 Manage a narcissist

They're Not Likely to Change

But what if they become a better person? Everyone deserves a second chance. One of the reasons why people tend to find it difficult to cut a narcissist out is because of the idea that people change. While it is true that people can change, you need to understand the context that narcissists live in.

These people reject criticism, believe they're always right, and aggressively defend their stance against anyone, regardless of their relationship to that person. They simply loathe being told that they're wrong in any way, and they'll fight violently to make sure that they get things their way.

With very poor insight as to what they do and how they act, it's very difficult to tap into a narcissist and make them see the reality of their life or their behaviour. That's why those who suffer from the personality disorder and those with severe tendencies rarely ever voluntarily seek counseling and treatment.

When it all comes right down to it, anyone who tries to point out their flaws is simply jealous. So, it's impossible for these people to change, no matter how many members of their family and their friends you're able to rally up to serve the truth.

All that said, you shouldn't expect a narcissist to change. If they show signs of change, it's likely not to change at all, but a ploy to get you to soften up and then abuse you once again with their controlling, tyrannical need for dominance and admiration.

You Will Look Bad

While it's possible to cut ties with a narcissist while dealing minimal damage, you need to understand that there is no such thing as a completely clean exit strategy. This is especially true if you share more connections like friends, family members, and co-workers with the narcissist you want to break off with.

For example, a man who grew up with a narcissistic father might try to limit his interactions with his parent in order to give himself some freedom to move, live, and decide for himself. His childhood friend who grew up knowing his father might notice the distance and ask, "Why don't you visit your dad anymore?"

Explaining his reality might help him release pent-up emotions. But because his friend grew up only scratching the surface of his dad's personality by sharing light conversation, seeing him at the family home, and hearing stories about him from other people, he might think the son is being rash and unreasonable.
"He's the only dad you'll ever have." Sure, that is true. But from the perspective of someone who's been sapped of energy all his life, it seems like a small price to pay.

Remember, most people around you grew up in well-adjusted homes with parents, relatives, and friends who likely weren't narcissistic. So, they won't be able to empathize with you because they don't know what it's like to deal with someone with narcissistic tendencies.

On top of that, you might also incur a few scratches to your image because of the narcissist's natural tendency to drop secrets to other people. Once they notice what you're trying to do, or if your attempt to break it off ends in an explosive argument, be prepared to handle the isolation.

Narcissists will divide and conquer, scratching you out of the image and brainwashing all your common friends and relatives to believe the worst about you. This means that some of the most important people in your life might cut you out as well, because of the nasty stories that might start spreading soon after you break off the relationship.

It's Going to Hurt

This ultimately depends on the depth of your relationship with the narcissist, but in most cases, it can definitely be painful to work away those knots that bind you together.

Discovering that someone is a narcissist especially if it's been years since you became a part of each other's lives can be an emotional journey.

It takes a lot of time and effort to unravel all the layers of their personality, and you might feel shocked when former truths are suddenly revealed to be absolute lies. For instance, a child who once thought that his parent's restrictive nature was well-meaning might be surprised to learn that it was actually an exercise of control.

As you go through the process and unpack more and more of the truths in front of you that weren't obvious at the start, you might feel shame, betrayal, and anger. Don't worry – it's all part of the healing. Just keep your head held high and remind yourself that none of their behaviours define who you are as a person.

Can You Live with Them?

Can you imagine completely isolating yourself from someone you've known and loved for years? How about someone who you consider to be a part of yourself, like a romantic partner or a family member?

No doubt, dealing with even just the idea of losing someone you love out of your own volition might seem too difficult to bear - even if that person makes you feel negatively about yourself and the world around you. So many end up asking - is it possible to live with a narcissist?

For those of us who don't want to inflict pain on others or endure pain themselves, there's the option of simply suffering through the emotional, mental, and possibly even physical abuse. This is typically seen as the 'easy way out' because it eliminates the need for confrontation, and thus reduces the chances of destroying relationships. If you're particularly invested in the relationship you have with a specific narc, then the idea of leaving might not even cross your mind at all.

But is it really that easy?

When you consider things from the perspective of the now, you might say that avoiding a narcissist can only cause more harm, but the opposite is actually true. Called energy vampires, keeping these dangerous people around you could consume your emotional and mental health. They can make you doubt yourself and force you to put your needs on hold.

Over the long run, you might find yourself sputtering and struggling to keep a smile on your face. You might feel fearful of their criticism and their explosive temper.

Individuals who stay in narcissistic relationships all their lives claim a feeling of loss of identity, and have been reported to manifest early signs of depression.

What you need to realize is that while it might seem ideal to simply 'ignore' their behaviour and maintain your presence in each other's lives instead of cutting them out permanently, their behaviour will make them difficult to be with down the line.

As humans, there's only so much we can take, and you need to understand that your energy is limited. Once that vampire saps you dry, then you'll start to experience burn out.

What does a person look like after years of suffering through a narcissist's abuse? Here's a sneak peek at the possibilities:

- **Void of an independent identity.** Narcissists crave control, and will do anything and everything they can to make sure the people close to them manifest the traits and qualities they believe are worthy of praise. Of course, if you're going to be closely associated to them, you're going to have to look and act a certain way so they won't feel 'embarrassed' to have you hanging around.

Their unreasonable desire for perfection will generate unrealistic expectations for the people around them. If these expectations are not met, then they resort to criticizing and insulting the person who failed them.

If you're choosing to stay, then you need to know how this can affect your own identity. Victims of narcissistic abuse find themselves constantly living in anxiety and fear, wondering when the next explosive episode might happen. Not wanting to be the reason for it, they submit themselves to the desires of the narcissist.

This mentality of 'peace at any price' compromises the person's identity. They have to dress, act, and behave the way the narcissist wants them to, causing them to give up their own unique preferences and qualities.

Over the long haul, a victim might completely lose him or herself, unable to make decisions without first consulting the narcissist for approval.

- **The role of the scapegoat**. If you've chosen to live with a narcissist, then you need to be prepared to be their scapegoat. These individuals will feel upset and angry more often than not, and it often doesn't really matter who did what - they'll lash out at anyone within proximity.

For you, this means possibly taking the brunt for a variety of issues that weren't even your fault to begin with. If you made even just a minor mistake within the same time frame, then the narcissist might use that as fuel to justify their anger at you.

So a wife who just happens to overcook her narcissistic husband's dinner a little more than he prefers might find him unreasonably yelling at her after a frantic, stressful day at work.

In these instances, your best defense would be to say you're sorry. Yes, even if you were not at fault. You need to adopt the role of the placate - the person who just does whatever their narcissistic contact wants in order to maintain peace.

- **Fluctuating treatment**. Today, the narcissist loves you. Tomorrow, they hate you with a burning passion. The way a narcissist treats you will never be set in stone, and they can flip that switch almost instantly depending on a variety of factors.

For instance, a mother of 5 might look at her eldest with stars in her eyes - he's the perfect son, the golden boy, and the standard to which all other children are compared. Everyone else is subpar and undeserving of love and affection.

Only when they match or exceed the eldest's performance are they deemed worthy of any sort of validation.

Unfortunately one day, the eldest comes home with a girl - his new love interest whom he wants to introduce to the family. The young lady is pleasant, respectful, and quiet, but she's just not quite beautiful enough for the mother's taste. So she acts withdrawn the whole evening, and even walks out as they all share dinner.

When the girl leaves, the mother confronts her son to tell him to break it off. But he's dead set, and expresses his genuine affection for his new girlfriend.

So his mother lashes out and calls him an ingrate. The next day, she ignores her eldest completely, and starts treating her second oldest son - who is without a romantic interest - as though he were the new golden boy.

Narcissists know that the people around them

crave their approval and affection because it's hard to come by.

So they will deliberately manipulate people by giving and taking their love whenever they see it necessary. If you act opposite to what they want, then the narcissist will withhold all care and affection until you come to your senses and act according to their preferences.

- **A painful lack of empathy**. Imagine attending a family gathering with your narcissistic partner. During the festivities, as everyone enjoys the food and company, one of the guests brings up their recent promotion. Not wanting to let the conversation dwell too far from herself, the narcissist rifles through her mind to find something she can talk about - related to the topic but with enough meat to make her look good.

She chooses to talk about the report you delivered at work which completely tanked. Your bosses were unimpressed and asked you to redo the whole thing, which your partner shares as if making a joke. To top it all off, she ends the story with "I tried to tell him what to do, but he just doesn't listen!"

She looks good, you look bad, and now

she managed to get people to ask her questions about her story, allowing her the opportunity to maintain all eyes on her.

So she wins. But you? You're left sitting in the corner, shaking your head in embarrassment.

A narcissist wouldn't know what empathy was even if it ran them over. They can't 'put themselves in others' shoes' and only really see things how they want to.

In a lot of ways, you can liken them to a horse with blinders on - they can't see anywhere around them, only what's in front of them.

Living with a narcissist means suffering through the embarrassment and humiliation that comes hand in hand with their need for attention. They will exploit your secrets even if you're right there to hear them do it, as long as it means being able to keep the spotlight for a little longer.

- **Exploiting your unique vulnerabilities**. Perhaps one of the hardest things to cope with when you continue to live with the energy vampire in your life is their strategy of exploiting unique vulnerabilities. They know where it hurts, and they'll jab their finger into that gaping wound if it means showing you that they're truly upset at you.

Take Anne for example, who decided to stay with her narcissistic husband despite his emotional abuse. She has adapted the 'peace at any price' syndrome, and expresses genuine distress whenever her husband manifests the slightest signs of anger. He knows that his wife would do anything to maintain his presence in her life, and he uses this to his advantage.

Recently, Anne was feeling pressured in the bedroom. Her husband was being too aggressive, asking her to do things that made her feel uncomfortable.

She expressed this to him and he whipped back saying that if she truly loved him, then she would have no problems with his request. Needless to say, her refusal to do as he pleased became the focal point of weeks' worth of marital arguments.

Months went by since, and Anne noticed her husband growing even more distant.

To her horror, she learned that he had been having an affair which he barely tried to conceal, leaving evidence of his exploits in places for Anne to find.

When she asked him about what she had seen, he gave her a cold look and simply said that this woman was willing to do what he asked. He blamed Anne for his actions and said that none of it would have happened if she had just listened and given him what he wanted.

Narcissists will turn to the most vile, hurtful, and immoral tactics if it means rubbing salt into their victim's open wounds. They won't think twice about hitting you where it hurts, and they'll likely do it even if it might be incredibly difficult to repair or impossible to undo.

- **An isolated life**. When you choose to stick with a narcissist, you basically write off everyone else in your life. You become an extension of the energy vampire, and thus you are technically his or her property. So your loyalty belongs to them, and you can't simply spend time with people you want to be with because they feel it compromises their control.

On top of that, the narcissist also isolates you in order to control what you share with other people. Being one of the few who's aware of who the narc is behind closed doors, they'll want to make sure that you don't end up spilling the beans and making them look bad to the people you might know.

If you end up in an argument with the narc, one of the first things they'll do is bad mouth you to your closest family and friends.

They'll play the victim and act as though you acted out of proportion and reason, earning them the sympathy of the parties they're trying to appeal to.

Once they have that secured, they'll warn these people that you're 'dangerous,' 'unstable,' and 'untrustworthy.' This creates a bias and pre-empts any attempts you might make to talk about your recent run-in with the narcissist. When you do decide to share what you've been through, the closest people in your life already have some idea - albeit askew - as to what happened. And so your story might not sell.

More often than not, you'll have to tread this lonely road all by yourself.
And you have to be ready to be left behind by some of the most important people in your life if you happen to make the mistake of arguing with the narc.

Now, it's worth asking - is it really worth it to keep a narcissist in your life?

Typically, people who choose to maintain the presence of an energy vampire struggle to see the truth. They continue believing that the initial impression the narcissist gave is who they really are, and that this hurtful behaviour is simply a phase.

What you need to remember is that narcissism is never a phase - it's a way of life.

That initial impression was a necessary step in their scheme to find victims and keep them where they are. By showing you something good at the start, you're baited into this toxic relationship and the narcissist wins at finding their supply.

At the end of the day, leaving the narc is always the smartest thing to do. Above all else, you need to think about your own well-being and mental health.

Sometimes, you will have to endure confrontation and pain, but if it's done in your best interest, then it might be worth it. Just remember to keep your own emotional health above all else, and guard your energy from those who seek to suck you dry and destroy your sense of self.

3.2 How do you know you are dealing with a narcissist

The need for attention

Narcissists not only want constant attention but will also demand the same. That behavior can be something as simple as constantly following you around the house, saying outrageous things to grab your attention, or asking you to do things for them.

Narcissists' wants for validation is as

constant as their need for attention. They require constant validation, and it doesn't count unless it comes from others. Even then, it doesn't mean much.

A narcissist's need for attention and validation is like a black hole that can never be filled. You can channel all your positivity, support, and attention, but even then, it will not fulfill the narcissist's need. Regardless of how much and how often you tell a narcissist about your love and admiration for them, it will never be enough. A narcissist's psyche is such that he truly believes that he is incapable of being loved by others. In spite of the façade of self-absorption and a sense of grandiose, a narcissist is often insecure and afraid of never being able to measure up. He craves praise and approval from others because it helps to bolster his fragile ego.

Extremely controlling

Narcissists are almost always disappointed with the way life turns out, so they try to do everything they can to control and shape it according to their wishes. They not only need to be controlled, but they demand that they must be in control. Their sense of entitlement and superiority only fuels their belief that they must be in control of everything. Not just that, narcissists will also have a specific storyline in their mind for every character in their life. They expect others to behave and react in the manner they have imagined in their mind. When this doesn't happen—in fact, it seldom does—it just makes narcissists feel unsettled and upset. They are incapable of predicting what will happen next since you are going "off-script."

So, don't be surprised if you notice that narcissists will often demand that you must speak and behave in a specific manner so that they can retain their sense of control. You are merely a character in the play that the narcissists are directing.

Narcissists fail to see that others are separate entities with their own thoughts and desires.

The unmistakable feeling of superiority

Narcissists tend to live in a two-dimensional world where everything is either black or white. Everyone and everything can be classified as good or bad, right or wrong, and superior or inferior. There exists a specific hierarchy in their minds, and they are obviously present in the top tier.

A narcissist will feel safe only when he thinks he is at the top. A narcissist always feels like he must be the absolute best; he must always be right and should be able to control everyone around him.

A narcissist also thinks people must always do things the narcissist's way.

It is quite interesting to note that a narcissist can also experience this feeling of superiority by being the absolute worst, the wrongest, or even the most upset.

If they feel like this, they tend to think that they are entitled to receive concern or empathy, and they may even think that they have the right to hurt others or demand an apology to make things right. A sense of absolute superiority and entitlement are amongst the defining traits of a narcissist.

Absence of boundaries

Narcissists are incapable of seeing where they end and where you begin. They are quite similar to toddlers.

They seem to think that everything belongs to them, that everyone thinks as they do, and that everyone wants the same things they do. In fact, narcissists will be quite shocked and affronted if they realize this isn't true.

If narcissists desire something from you, they will go to great lengths to get what they want. The narcissists can be extremely persistent in their quest for getting what they want from you or others.

Shrugs all responsibility

A narcissist does love to be in control, but he will never want to accept any responsibility for the turn of events unless everything goes the way he planned and the desired results are obtained.

When things don't proceed according to his plan or when he receives any criticism, the narcissist will conveniently shift all the responsibility and the blame onto others.

It has to be someone else's fault because narcissists are the epitome of perfection, at least, according to themselves.

Since they are perfect, if things don't go as planned, it must be someone else's fault. At times, the blame can be quite generalized—the police, the management, the teachers, the government, and so on. At times, the blame can be quite specific.

The narcissist might pick a specific individual to blame like his parents, the law, or even the judge. Usually, a narcissist tends to blame the person that he is quite close to.

To enable the fragile façade of perfection, a narcissist will often find someone to blame. If you happen to be the person the narcissist is closest to, then be prepared to take the blame.

You will be the safest person to blame because the chances of you leaving the narcissist are quite slim, and this makes him feel safe.

Desire for perfection

Narcissists have a desire for perfection and expect it from everyone and everything around them as well as themselves. They believe that they must be perfect, you must be perfect, and the events in life must be as expected and that their life needs to unfold precisely in the manner they envisioned. This exaggerated need for demanding the impossible is the reason why a narcissist often feels quite miserable and dissatisfied. Their constant need for perfection makes them complain constantly.

Complete lack of empathy

Only when you can understand others and can see where they are coming from will you be able to empathize with them. A narcissist cannot empathize with others. In fact, it is safe to say that narcissists are devoid of all empathy. They are selfish, self-absorbed, and self-centered.

These traits prevent a narcissist from ever being able to understand the feelings of others fully. Narcissists seldom give a conscious thought about what others might think or feel; after all, they expect others to think as they do. Also, a narcissist might not experience guilt or remorse and may rarely—if ever—apologize.

That said, narcissists are quite adept at identifying any alleged threats, anger, and rejection from others around him. At the same time, they are quite oblivious to the feelings and emotions of others around them.

They often misinterpret simple minute facial expressions and are biased while interpreting the same. Unless you display your emotions dramatically, narcissists are incapable of accurately assuming what you are experiencing. Even saying something as simple as "I love you" or "I am sorry" can backfire easily if the narcissists are in a foul mood. They might not believe you and will assume that your comment was an attack instead.

Apart from this, if your words and expressions are not in sync, the narcissists will respond incorrectly. It is the reason why most narcissists fail to understand sarcasm or jokes and think of them as a personal attack. Their inability to properly read body language is another reason why narcissists aren't empathetic. They cannot perceive emotions correctly, and they tend to misinterpret them. They also don't believe that you can think and act in a manner different from theirs.

Narcissists cannot understand the nature of feelings. They don't understand how feelings manifest. They believe their feelings are often the result of an external force or action. They don't realize that their feelings are a manifestation of their biochemistry, their thoughts, and their perceptions.

Simply put, narcissists believe you are responsible for what they feel, especially all the negative ones. They come to this conclusion because you deviated from their plan or because you made them feel insecure. So, the only logical recourse in a narcissist's mind is to blame you. This apparent lack of empathy certainly makes it quite difficult to establish a true and meaningful relationship with a narcissist.

Constant anxiety

Anxiety is the constant feeling that something terrible is either happening or is bound to happen. Some might display their anxiety by constantly talking about all the bad that's about to happen while others hide or repress their anxiety.

However, most narcissists tend to shift their anxiety onto those they are close to by accusing them of being unsupportive and selfish. All this is a means of projecting and transferring the anxiety they experience to make themselves feel better. By making others feel worse, they feel stronger and better.

Reasoning proves to be futile

You might have probably tried to reason or use logic while trying to make a narcissist understand the negative effects his actions had on you. You might think that if the narcissist can understand the hurt the actions caused you, he will change. However, your explanation probably made no sense to the narcissist.

He is the only one who is aware of what he feels and thinks. Even if a narcissist says he understands what you are saying, it is highly unlikely that he does.

So, a narcissist will often make most of his decisions solely based on what he thinks and feels about a specific topic. He needs a sports car because of the way he feels while driving it and not because it is a good choice. If he is bored or upset, he will want to shift, change jobs, or even end a relationship. Not just this, the narcissist will also expect you to go along with his ideal "solution" because it is logical to him. If you don't accept the "solution" willingly or refuse to do something, he will only resent you.

Suppressed fears

Narcissists' lives are motivated and fueled by fear. Most of the fears that narcissists have are often deeply buried or even suppressed. They live in constant fear of being ridiculed and rejected by others.

They might be scared about losing their fortune, being emotionally attacked, physically threatened, being seen as inadequate, or being deserted. All these things make it almost impossible for narcissists ever fully to trust others.

In fact, the more intimate the bond is, the less the narcissist will trust you. Narcissists are often scared of intimacy and vulnerability.

They fear these things because they think that once others can see their imperfections, they will be rejected or abandoned. Regardless of all the reassurance narcissists receive, it will not make a difference.

Their failure in accepting their imperfections makes it difficult for them to believe that others can accept them for who they are. They cannot trust the love they receive and will come up with different ways to test others and push them to their breaking point.

Inability to be vulnerable

Because narcissists are incapable of understanding feelings, lack empathy, and have a constant urge for self-protection, they cannot truly love, accept, or connect with others. They cannot view the world from anyone else's perspective except their own.

They are emotionally deaf toward others, and this leads to loneliness.

In fact, this makes them quite needy. When they feel dissatisfied with one relationship, they will abandon it faster than rats abandoning a sinking ship. They constantly look for someone who can offer them sympathy and go along with everything they say and do.

Not a team player

If one cannot understand others, the said person cannot exhibit any thoughtful or cooperative behavior. How will others feel? If I do this, will it make me as well as others happy? What effect will this have on the relationship? These are some questions that a narcissist is incapable of answering or even thinking about. So, it is obvious that a narcissist cannot be a good team player.

Constant division

A narcissist's personality is often divided into two parts: good and bad. This makes a narcissist split everything in his relationships into two: good and bad. Any negative thought or behavior will be blamed on his partners or others, and he will take the credit for all things good and positive.

A narcissist will also vehemently deny his negative words and acts while incessantly accusing others of being critical or judgmental.

Apart from this, narcissists are quite good at categorizing their memories into two extremes: wonderful ones and horrible ones. Their failure to realize that life is a mix of all things good and bad prevents them from seeing, understanding, and combining these two views.

Narcissists are incapable of seeing, feeling, and remembering the positive as well as the negative aspects of any given situation. They are capable of only dealing with one perspective: only theirs.

Repressed feelings

Narcissists seldom experience any guilt because they believe they are always right and cannot fathom that their behavior might affect others. However, narcissists tend to experience a lot of shame. Shame is the feeling that there is something terribly and irreparably wrong about who you are. Hidden deep in some repressed part of the narcissists' psyche resides all their feelings of insecurities and fears—all the traits the narcissists are trying to hide from the world and themselves.

They are often deeply ashamed of all those thoughts and feelings, which are rejected by them. Narcissists have a primal need to hide their vulnerabilities because if they don't, then it will shatter their illusion of self-esteem. These things make it quite difficult for a narcissist ever fully to be transparent.

3.3 Can narcissists change?

Yes, Narcissists can change. However, it is quite a process. Even if they do realize that they have a problem, much of the time, their opinion of themselves is so inflated or they generally lack the capacity for empathy such that they simply don't seem to care at all. In these cases, people often won't ever seek any sort of "true" help as it were for their narcissistic personality disorder.

The route that this leaves psychotherapists and psychiatrists is such that they need to recognize and fill that void by working around the issue if the patient ever does go for help.

Another unfortunate truth of narcissistic personality disorder is that most patients who have narcissistic personality disorder don't have their disorder discovered voluntarily. Indeed, most people who suffer from this disorder have their disorder discovered because they are going for another condition.

There is a high rate of psychological comorbidity between narcissistic personality disorder and other mental illnesses such as depression, anxiety, bipolar depression, and related illnesses. Individuals with narcissistic personality disorder will often also suffer from substance abuse disorders, with a particular predilection towards cocaine.

When one thinks of treating a mental disorder, their first thought generally is whether or not medication is available for something, and whether or not medication could be considered a viable treatment course.

In the specific case of narcissistic personality disorder, medication doesn't seem to be particularly useful. This is mostly because narcissistic personality disorder is due to such a huge combination of environmental factors as well as due to the fact that in people with narcissistic personality disorder, the parts of the brain related to functions such as empathy and compassion are actually shrunken. All of these combine to yield the fact that in terms of practical medication therapy, there are few avenues.

Historically, people with narcissistic personality disorder were treated with psychoanalysis. The Freudians would follow this model and attempt to recover important parts of a person's psyche through the purported connection between various life events and the Freudian assessment of youth and its impact on later mental disorders.

In the sixties, the trend changed a bit. Focus shifted towards using psychoanalytic psychotherapy in order to address patients who have narcissistic personality disorder. Several different strategies have been outlined since then for addressing patients who have narcissistic personality disorder, with a general focus on changing the overall mindset of the person who has it.

Do note that in the case of comorbid disorders, such as depression, bipolar disorder, or anxiety, some improvement may be noted through the treatment of these satellite disorders.

Mental illnesses tend to have stacking effects and will synergize with one another in order to worsen each other. However, as stated before, these cannot be expected to cure a patient's narcissism in and of themselves. Rather, a specific focus is given to building a strong bond between the therapist and the patient and then using this bond in order to get the patient to both feel more empathetic and more reflective of their actions.

Some traits of narcissists are more difficult to change than others. For example, while one may have luck breaking a patient down and starting to understand what led to the development of their narcissism, especially in the case of a formed defense mechanism, this specific procedure is much more difficult than, let's say, trying to get the patient to use their ability to manipulate people and situations and use their unique view of both themselves and the world in order to benefit the people around them rather than themselves.

In this capacity, part of the narcissist's psychotherapy will consist of attempting to get them to use some kind of reflection skills and then use the skills that their personality disorder has endowed them with in order to help others.

This is not to glorify the traits the patient has developed but rather to help them develop a sense of empathy towards others as well as to help them in using these for an overall "good" purpose. It accepts that the traits exist while using them to the patient's advantage and the advantage of the people around them rather than using them in a wholly selfish manner.

One must also recognize the specific difficulties of a therapist in treating narcissistic personality disorder. For example, narcissists often will not react well to criticism. This presents a unique difficulty to the therapist because they likely won't be able to approach the narcissistic tendencies directly.

In a large capacity, the handling of narcissistic personality disorder from a psychotherapeutic perspective necessitates the building of an extremely strong alliance between the therapist and the patient and requires likewise extremely gentle treading on the part of the therapist. Otherwise, they may end up undoing much of the progress that they actually accomplish.

However, the therapist can help the narcissist to work on their worse qualities, like anger, unnecessary annoyance, overall impatient demeanour, and rage.

In working on these, the therapist also works on the worse reactions of the patient in terms of defense mechanisms in terms of their narcissistic qualities. This gives them a much better window of attack.

Do be aware, too, that psychotherapy may not always be an effective route for the treatment of narcissistic personality disorder. It is only as effective as the patient will allow it to be. If they are unable to take the feedback of the therapist without offense or perceiving it as being largely pointless, baseless, or generally incorrect, then there's not much of a leg for the therapist to stand on.

It's not unusual for a patient with narcissistic personality disorder to reject the therapist's analyses, especially if they're hypercritical and/or the therapist doesn't have much experience treading as carefully as a narcissist requires them to tread.

In place of psychotherapy, some people with narcissism will benefit instead from pursuing group therapy. People with narcissistic personality disorder may find the comments of their peers more readily accessible and, indeed, more easy to digest than those of medical professionals. Group therapy can be especially useful for somebody with narcissistic personality disorder because even though they lack much of the empathy required to fully empathize with the people in the sessions, they still will be able to experiment with the idea of interpersonal boundaries, as well as develop a better understanding of trust and accepting criticism.

More than that, being around other narcissists may allow them to recognize the behaviours of others in themselves, which can be a rather major step forward.

In the end, there are few people more difficult to treat than a narcissist. This is because narcissists are very unique; they are some of the patients least likely to admit that they have a problem.

Most narcissists would never go to a therapist for the direct purpose of having them treat their narcissism. Narcissistic personality disorder is normally caught as a comorbidity and doesn't often prompt patients to seek help on its own. Because of this, it has to be attacked indirectly by the therapists, who are particularly challenged by this disorder. The lack of an effective medication plan other than just treating those disorders which appear to be comorbid with the narcissism means that much of the remaining effective treatment lies in different therapy paths. However, not all hope is lost. For patients who are willing to develop themselves through therapy, whether it be psychotherapy or group therapy or both, a marked improvement is usually noted in the patient's ability to empathize with others.

By the end of their sessions, patients normally have made a quite large improvement in terms of their interpersonal effectiveness and their general ability to reflect on themselves and their tendencies.

3.4 How not to be overwhelmed by a narcissist

Narcissists are born charmers and manipulators, so it might be very difficult trying to control a narcissist but it's not an impossible task. Doesn't matter if it's a friend or a partner, if you want to help them control their behaviour there are various steps that you can take. The first step is to realize that it's you who is in control now and not the narcissist.

Further, you have to use this advantage to your benefit, try to get on the good side of the narcissist. This is the only way that they'll even consider listening to you. Moving on, you can help them by taking to them and showing them the correct way. The most important part of controlling a narcissist it to be in control yourself, if you lose your temper at any time it'll only result in the narcissist withdrawing back.

Being on the good side of the Narcissist

Listen to them

Narcissists love praise and attention, so the first step to gaining their favor is to pay attention to what they are saying. Listen closely to whatever they're trying to say, don't just hear it but reply to them with more praise and positive comments. Be prepared to be their center of attention, they'll be constantly nagging you to listen to them and you will be on the receiving end of the conversation almost always.

It is a tough job because it gets boring listening to one person talk about their achievements and what not but if you really want to control them, this is the only solution.

Narcissists can easily know if you're lying to them or just putting up a show to make it look like you're listening, so don't just smile at them but actually listen to what they are saying. Give positive feedback; make them think that you really care about each and every detail of their life. Narcissists also react aggressively if they think that they are being cheated so look at their reactions if you think that they're starting to know that you're faking it, you have to start pretending better.

Sincerely praise them

Narcissists already have a huge ego and they love nothing more than hearing people praise them, so that's your cue to give them genuine praise. Find their best qualities, achievements and anything else you can complement them on.

If they ever react negatively to

something make sure that you never bring that topic up, it's because they are insecure about that particular topic and will react negatively if forced to talk about it.

The more attention you give to the narcissist, the more chances you have on ending up on their good side. Always talk to them, go over to their house and spend time with them, be needy and clingy and constantly message them. All of these will make them think that you're someone who likes to pay attention to them. When you're praising something about them, make sure that it is in front of others, that's because the more people that hear about their greatness, the more their ego increases. Narcissists are also obsessive in terms for portraying their best qualities to people.

If you genuinely praise too many of their qualities, then these are the qualities that the narcissist will reciprocate for you thinking that you love these qualities.

So, make sure that when you offer them praise it's not too much, or it'll be you who is in trouble. Take their best quality that you love and constantly praise them about it such as how charming they are or how sweet they are.

This way you get to praise them without being forced to deal with a quality you do not like.

Don't think that you're escalating their personality disorder, most adult narcissist have already reached a point where their ego is at max and cannot be increased further.

Build a personal connection

The only way to talk properly to a narcissist is by using the 'I' language. Most narcissists are extremely defensive and aggressive; if you criticize them then they will probably try to push the blame on you.

It's impossible to not have a fight with a narcissist, there will be some sort of disagreement and it will lead to misunderstanding. It is important that you be prepared for such a scenario to make sure that your connection doesn't deteriorate. The only solution to this is to approach them personally and try to build a strong connection with them. There will of course be heated arguments, you won't back down that easily and nor will the narcissist. Now, it's important that you use the correct language with the narcissist or the situation can go out of hand. Paraphrase your words to make sure that you use the 'I' language, make sure that they understand that you're a human too and have feelings.

This is a simple technique to generate empathy in the narcissist; it will help you in your argument and also help you later on.

The 'I' language makes sure that you do not say something rash, narcissists are extremely prone to show aggressive behaviour but when you approach them personally, they'll be more likely to listen to you. As an example, if you got into an argument with a narcissist and you feel bad about it then say, 'I feel bad that I fought with you' instead of saying 'You made me realize that we shouldn't have fought'. Narcissists don't believe in apologies so when you reach them on a personal level they are more likely to listen to you.

Don't accept blame

Narcissists are very good at the blame game that is, blaming others for all of their mistakes. You need to make sure that you don't easily accept the blame and don't blame the narcissist either. Use a language that depicts your dedication towards not arguing with the narcissist and keeping good relations. Narcissists are extremely fragile and if you blame them for anything, they'll reciprocate the same behaviour and blame you.

The end result will be that you both will be exhausted since none of you accept that you were wrong and it will turn into a huge fight. As stated before, the first step is to maintain good relations with the narcissist, if you take such a step, it will inevitably lead to a fight that will destroy your relations. So, if you really want to control a narcissist make sure that you do not enter the blame game.

A clear example of perfect behaviour in such a situation is to not say 'You're the one who is at fault' but rather say that 'I don't know how this problem occurred and I am not okay to take the blame for it'.

It's very important that you pick the correct words when dealing with a narcissist; they listen very carefully and at the first hint of blame with lash out. This example shows the perfect behaviour because you did not accept the blame and give control to the narcissist but at the same you maintained good relations by not blaming the narcissist. For example, suppose you meet a narcissist at work and you both are working on a project, now by mistake some error popped up.

The narcissist would obviously try to blame you for the mistake, but you shouldn't reply with 'No, this is not my fault, you are the one to blame' but rather explain to the narcissist that it's not either of your fault that there was an error since you both were responsible for the project. The narcissist will quickly take this option because they are not being blamed and will not feel insecure due to the same.

Chapter 4

Defend yourself against narcissists

4.1 What are the causes of Narcissistic Personality Disorder?

When looking at the statistics, the figure of approximately one percent of the population having narcissistic personality disorder seems eerily high—uncomfortably high, perhaps. By now, we've built up a broader and stronger idea of who is normally affected by it. As we can see, narcissistic personality disorder certainly doesn't discriminate, though there is a number of criteria that make somebody more likely to have the disorder, and it does seem to occur more commonly in men than in women.

Despite looking at the people that narcissistic personality disorder occurs within—or, rather, the groups which seem to present with his disorder the most—we still haven't looked at a huge number of the root causes.

The prime focus of this chapter is going to be looking at the different causes of narcissistic personality disorder and what can actually lead to somebody developing this horrible disorder.

The exact causes of narcissistic personality disorder are currently unknown. There are a number of indirect suppositions as to what causes it, and all of these culminate into what is the general modern vision of what leads to the development of this disorder.

The going consensus on what leads to the development of narcissistic personality disorder is that it's ultimately a combination of genetic, social, environmental, and biological factors.

The exact role that each of these plays in the development of this disorder can vary depending upon the individual and the exact subtype of the disorder developed can vary equally as much. That is to say, there is no sure cocktail of causes that will lead to the development of one specific subtype or another.

In order to dive into the big question of "why does this happen?" a bit more, we're going to be looking at this one-by-one in order to come to a firmer understanding on what causes narcissistic personality disorder.

Firstly, let's look at the genetic aspect:

there is a lot of evidence that the disorder itself can be inherited. The existence of a family member with the disorder makes it far more likely that a given individual will develop the disorder themselves. Studies performed on twins have been rather conducive to showing that there is an inheritable aspect to the disorder.

It can be difficult, though, to determine how much of this is because of the person growing up with somebody who has the disorder—for example, if somebody's father were to have narcissistic personality disorder.

This no doubt would lead to the child taking in that influence and being, to one extent or another, impacted by the disorder and more likely to develop it themselves.

In this case, narcissistic personality disorder could be seen as both a genetic and a social disorder.

Beyond the genetic factors, there are a number of different environmental factors at play as well. Here, we're going to be looking at both the social and environmental catalysts to the development of narcissistic personality disorder.

These are largely thought to play the biggest part in the development of the disorder—larger than either the genetic or biological causes, though with environment and biology likely playing equal parts or with environment only slightly weighted in favor compared to biology.

One of the largest catalysts for the development of narcissistic personality disorder is when a child learns manipulative behavior from either their parents or their friends. Manipulative parents are extremely common, and unfortunately, manipulative parenting styles weren't condemned for a rather long time. With developmental psychology and emotional abuse only becoming topics that were largely discussed in the second half of the 20th century, what results is the fact that there are still some rather ancient parenting styles that are incredibly unhealthy.

More than that, it doesn't just come down to the parenting style; it also comes down to a person's general way of life. It's unfortunate, but due to the way that manipulative behavior works, it's possible for a manipulative person to surround themselves with people they can manipulate and never have to change their behavior. Because of this, they could teach this to a child as the norm.

With attitudes on parenting largely shifting in the twenty-first century, this problem will hopefully become less and less prominent as people start to discuss things such as mental and emotional abuse more and they become more acceptable topics of discourse. Until then, this will remain a rather prominent catalyst.

This goes hand-in-hand with another catalyst for the development of narcissistic personality disorder: emotional abuse in childhood.

Manipulative behavior and emotional abuse aren't necessarily one and the same, but they do often go hand-in-hand. In the latter case, one may develop narcissistic personality disorder as a defense mechanism or coping mechanism.

These can be some of the hardest cases to deal with from a psychological perspective because dealing with them means dealing with a much deeper trauma. This is compared to just trying to make people rationalize their position in other individuals who didn't have to endure emotional abuse as a child.

That isn't to say, though, that a narcissist may necessarily have developed this as a defense or coping mechanism.

In fact, many people develop the disorder as a result of things which happen to them in other ways. For example, a lot of people like to take the post that there's no such thing as excessive praise for a child. However, when a child is developing, many of the actions which occur to them—if they stick out in any way—will be intensely formative and cemented into their brain forever unless they make a very active attempt to unlearn them.

If somebody is excessively praised, they may develop the idea that they're unable to do any wrong. This happens often with single parents who don't wish to lose the respect or adoration of their child, unfortunately, and I've seen it pop up in quite a few cases of such.

Likewise, if a child is excessively criticized, they may develop narcissistic personality disorder as a defense mechanism.

If people tell somebody all the time that they're exceptionally beautiful or talented with little basis in reality or little realistic, earthbound feedback in response to the praise, they're at risk for the development of narcissistic personality disorder.

If people overvalue somebody or indulge them too often, that person becomes far more likely to develop the disorder.

In essence, the mind desires some sort of equilibrium in terms of its interactions with other people. It does whatever it can to reach out for this equilibrium and seek it out. Believe it or not, not all minds are equally resilient and able to so handily endure some of the stresses or excesses of life. In other words, a lot of what causes narcissistic personality disorder can be seen as over-parenting. Someone who excessively gives praise, criticism, or manipulates their child puts their child at risk for the development of narcissistic personality disorder.

Parents who are narcissists themselves will often use their children as a means of self-validation and force their narcissistic behaviors onto their children.

This lead, generally, to either resentment or the development of Stockholm syndrome. In the former case, people may drop contact with their parents or limit contact as much as possible. In the latter, they will often model themselves after their parents.

In terms of biological factors which correspond to the development of this disorder, there isn't a whole lot of research to work with.

As I said earlier, finding finite study opportunities for narcissistic personality disorder can be difficult. However, what studies have been done have shown that the areas of the brain having to do with empathy, emotion, and compassion generally are not nearly as large as they are in neurotypical people or people without mental disorders.

One question many people might ask while reading this is whether or not they can tell if their child is a narcissist. If you picked this book up in the first place because you're worried that your child may have this disorder, then I've got a relatively disappointing answer for you: your guess is as good as mine.

The thing is that while one of the things linked to the development of narcissistic personality disorder is being overly sensitive as an infant, this is one of the only signs that one has for the development of narcissistic personality disorder until adolescence is reached. There are also a number of oversensitive children that don't grow up to have this disorder. This means that in terms of a concrete answer, we're a little bit at a loss.

If you're worried that your child may be a narcissist, then review your parenting style and take a little look into your family history. If there are other people who show signs of narcissistic personality disorder, or if you tend to excessively praise your child without realistic feedback or excessively criticize them, then you may have a narcissist on your hands. However, many children and teens will show the symptoms of narcissism as a passing phase before finally growing out of it. Their brains are maturing, and they have a lot to learn about the world. Depending on how young they are, just address the manner in a reasonable way relative to their age.

If you're seriously concerned or your child shows an excessive amount of the symptoms, it may not be a bad idea to set up a trip to a child psychiatrist in order to have them professionally evaluated.

If they are found to have narcissism or any related psychiatric disorder, your psychiatrist will work with you and your child in order to chart a path forward.

4.2 How dangerous can a narcissist become?

Devaluation risk.
Being in a relationship with a narcissist, can be stable. They might devalue you if you made any big difference according to their judgement. Narcissists consider other non-existent by cutting connections with them and devaluing them.

This explains why being in a relationship with a narcissist even when things are going on well.

Strong desire for vengeance.

Narcissists seek revenge than normal people because they have big egos. They can deal a fatal blow with someone who humiliated or hurt them, not only trying to seek revenge. Completely crushing the person who hurt or humiliated them, makes them feel so good.

Replacing you at any time

You can be replaced by a narcissist at any time. They can replace you as soon as they start believing that you are not enough. They do this without even negotiating with you.

Making you feel worthless

A narcissist is good at demeaning people. They will say many things with the intent of making you feel worthless and believe you me, they are good at doing this.

No negotiation

When a narcissist is hurt, they do not negotiate. However, they immediately act and they will not question you for treating them badly. They focus on revenging without giving a room to negotiate with you.

Full of rage

A narcissist will get hurt very easily because they have a big ego. Anything that comes their way can easily hurt them and this quickly gets them into rage as they see they are being hurt.

Blocking You

A narcissist can immediately block you if they believe that you do not respect them by the way you behave. This is because you they feel that they can't cope with you.

4.3 10 tips to defend yourself from narcissists (Details on tips in message below)

Don't hope to change them

It is the number one rule when dealing with narcissists. They are convinced that they are always right, they have no self-critical capacity and they just can't put themselves in others' shoes.

They tend to manipulate you by giving you feelings of guilt, anger, fear and insecurity. Establish a relationship of psychological subjection. The change in them will never occur.

Therefore, it is useless for you to try to argue with them and waste energy unnecessarily. To live with a narcissist, you must act on yourself. And change your attitude towards them to put up with them. The hard reality here is that it's impossible to change someone else, and trying will only hurt you. What you can start with is changing the way you see the situation.

For example, you can view your interactions with the narcissistic person as a way to train your mind in areas of self-control, patience, and general focus. Since listening to a narcissist at work can be so draining, this is a great chance to improve yourself.

Choose freedom.

Hyper-controlling narcissists use different techniques to keep you at their mercy. They leverage a sense of duty or gratitude, they make you feel guilty. Anything to force you to agree with them. Instead, learn to react independently of them, accepting their disapproval or anger. If you get dominated by another person, you betray yourself. Then choose the freedom that, besides being a right, is also a responsibility.

By sacrificing it, you would lose your own

identity. No one can live a satisfying life by following the tenets of another person.

Choosing freedom helps you live a life without stress. A narcissist does not like losing an argument and therefore, it is impossible to keep on arguing with them even when you are right. This way, you are good to go.

Keep your expectations low.

Passive-aggressive narcissists are elusive and evasive, they tend to postpone commitments and not keep promises. They show friendly, but don't act like friends. They do not openly discuss problems. They assert their will by behaving passively, that is, without ever cooperating with others. They are very frustrating. How to react? You must keep your expectations low.

The less you rely on them, the less disappointed you will be. In this way you will not authorize their behaviour irresponsible, but you will deal with reality. You must learn to accept them as they are. Remember the first rule: they will never change! When you are dealing with someone like this, having high expectations of them is only setting yourself up for disappointment.

Part of realistically assessing the situation is realizing that they are going to care about themselves first and foremost, and others second. They'll always think of themselves first and you should therefore have little, if any, expectations from them.

Don't pay attention to their justifications.

It is never their fault. If you try to criticize them, know that you will only get a boomerang effect. The remarks you will make to them will fall on you.

Narcissists have little capacity for introspection and have a strong need to feel special, so they will not recognize that they were wrong. You will never be able to prove them the opposite. So don't listen to their "reasons", continue on your way.

Get used to doing without their blessing. Being wrong is never a thing for them and they will spend a lot of time trying to justify how they are right.

Don't protect them.

It can often happen that they ask you not to talk about your problems to others. They must maintain an irreproachable image at all costs. Being silent, they think they can continue to treat you with arrogance.

It occurs particularly in couple relationships. It is not up to them to decide how much of your life you will want to share with another person. By continuing to protect the narcissists by following their rules instead of yours, you will do nothing but prolong your unhappiness. Do you want to always be unhappy? I guess not. If you protect them, you will continue suffering alone.

Be resolute in your decisions.

Narcissists often try to manipulate you using your guilt. They take advantage of their capacity for empathy and compassion, feelings that are foreign to them. To defend yourself, you must then balance this empathic tendency of yours with firm determination. The complaints of narcissists must not take over your decisions. Give priority to your common sense and your legitimate self-defense instinct. Stick with what you decide as they can easily try to manipulate you and make you feel guilty.

Use assertive anger.

Narcissists inevitably provoke anger.

It is wrong to let oneself be overcome by anger, but also to repress it because it is deposited in a fold of the personality and damages it causing depression, anxiety, resentment, cynicism, self-confidence ...

A positive way to express anger is assertiveness instead. This is how we defend our beliefs and show respect for others. Set aside aggression, speak firmly and remain consistent with the decision taken. In this way, anger will be used constructively to make you feel better, without expecting anything in return from narcissists.

Stop justifying your choices.

Once you have made your decision showing that you are adamant, avoid justifying your choices. Faced with the stubbornness of narcissists, who would like to continue to manipulate you, the dispute could never end.

Moreover, those who give themselves too much to rationalize their choices suggest the idea of not being so sure and of being able to change decision in case of insistence. A narcissist will never let you win, so your justification does not matter to them. Don't fall into this trap!

Be humble, don't become like them. Egoism generates selfishness.

If you are dealing with narcissists, be careful not to let yourself be conditioned to the point of becoming like them. We all have an innate selfish tendency and the risk is to start treating the narcissist in a disrespectful way. At this point the instinct of self-defense becomes self-centred.

To avoid this, we need to focus on humility. Indeed, those who are authentically humble are psychologically confident and do not need to take others to their side. He does not want to be overbearing towards others, but at the same time does not allow others to be against him. Egoism may slowly turn you int a narcissist! When you are humble you are able to control yourself and avoid becoming like them.

Forgive.

The positive aspects of forgiveness are manifold. It makes you free to focus on more important priorities than anger.

It encourages you not to get obsessed by those who wronged you anymore.

It allows you to look to the future. You cannot control the behaviours and choices of another person, but with forgiveness you can learn to accept and tolerate narcissists for what they are. More so, forgiveness gives you a peace of mind which is very important

Chapter 5

In a relationship with a narcissist

5.1 The phases of relationships with narcissists

Love phase

It begins in the cloud of love and usually too good to be true. Note being used to much admiration, but after some time you feel it's okay and are convinced you have found someone you connect with, with your dreams and beliefs.

And usually, after a short term, you are convinced he is the right person you put down the strict normal boundaries given that you have that feeling that the person you are with really adore you.

Devalue phase

During this stage, he starts to cut down your self-esteem, confidence and sense of you.

While experiencing it, you may not understand it, but his strategy is perfectly clear when you are the other side, which is for you to submit to his demands and him eroding your confidence and this becomes the beginning of him controlling you, you are extremely fortunate if you aren't married to him yet.

As things begin to change, he starts hating your close friends, family members whom he knows you love and have their interests at heart and makes your life uncomfortable. He even reaches a time and starts to criticize your appearance like the clothes you wear, make-up, hairstyle and insists you change those things he doesn't like.

Discard phase.

After obtaining what they wanted from the relationship, whether money, prestige or anything else he/she wanted, and has satiated his use, you will be discarded like a newspaper that has been used and replaced with a new one which can continue to feed their ego. If you can, get out of the relationship, cut off all contact and walk away with your head held high.

Recovery phase

If you are in the relationship with a narcissist, you need to start looking after yourself, you need relief from strain and stress of everything. Usually, words that have been fed to us over some period of time, remain with us. It's crucial to begin understanding and nurturing yourself that you are complete the way you are.

5.2 Can two narcissists be in a relationship?

The quick answer is yes. On a general look, narcissists couple don't seem like they can survive. If you imagine how nagging a narcissist can be and then imagine two of them together. It would be chaos! Right?

The surprising thing is that it can be the complete opposite. They can end up being a great couple and even do better than many couples out there.

When two narcissist people have same hobbies, they may get attracted to each other and be in a relationship. They love being on the spotlight and this would be perfect if they come together.

The downside of the narcissists relationships is that they don't last for the long-term. Despite this, narcissists can be attracted to other people who are not narcissists as potential mates for long-term relationship.

If you are not a narcissist, it will not be easy maintaining a relationship with a narcissist. However, you can learn on how to live with one and still be happy together as some narcissists are generous and kind.

5.3 In love with a narcissist? Best ways to make it work...

Can you make a relationship work when you are with a malignant narcissist? You could, but it's a lot of work and a lot of sacrifices because, like a fish out of water, a narcissist in a marriage is out of their element. After all, how can someone who sees themselves at the very center of the world, who's ever thought is about themselves, exist in the most communal of living situations where compromise is the only road to happiness?

Make no mistake, as far as the narcissist is concerned, this is their world, you just work here. What you might see as a partnership, they see as a monarchy and you are lucky to be a part of their court.

If you think you've got the wherewithal to force a change, or at least establish your own throne next to theirs, here are some things you need to do. Just remember, if you go ahead with this, there is going to be trouble.

Understand this: By doing these things, you are not harming your narcissist, nor are you betraying them. You are simply asserting your own personhood and rights as a fully realized human being.

Don't buy into the hype.

As a narcissist, they will see themselves and speak of themselves in grandiose terms and look for agreement from you to support their vision. Don't believe it and don't support it.

Remember that you're not their mommy.

If the relationship is new, don't build an expectation that you are the one to come in and take care of his every need. If you're already married, start pulling back in stages and make him handle his own issues.

Expect their Selfishness.

The narcissist is all about taking care of themselves, which means that your own needs could, and often will, go unanswered. Take a page from their book and take care of yourself as well. That way, you don't have to involve them unless you really want to.

Keep goals realistic and doable.

Your narcissist will set amazing goals for the two of you that are often far out of reach, like a month in Hawaii when your budget would only cover a week in Florida. You need to reign those in, find compromises, and try to help them achieve a more realistic goal. Don't allow the "Great" to become the enemy of the "Good."

Be there when it all goes to hell.

Remember those over-the-top goals? When they fail, you will find yourself with an exquisitely depressed individual desperate for any kind of validation. For your own sanity, if not for theirs, be nice and give it to them, but only as an emergency measure. In the long run, a dose of reality will be good for them.

Don't let yourself or others become tools.

Once your narcissist starts feeling a little better, they will begin to look for scapegoats to explain the failure and will try to enlist "help" to try again.

The fact that the goal was unrealistic or that they were not capable of seeing it through will never enter their minds. That said, they are more than likely to fail again, so the "help" they are trying to hijack will likely drain you and others of energy, money time, or other resources for absolutely no purpose. Try to find a compromise that would succeed, but don't let yourself or others get dragged into another boondoggle.

Control the Purse Strings.

Your narcissist sees themselves as the best, so they demand the best. The best car, house, food, computer, whatever it is, they want the very best money can buy.

The problem is that this expensive taste is usually paid-for by letting things slide elsewhere. Say you have a child on the way. While you are looking at nursery sets, cribs, car seats, diapers, bottles, paediatricians, your narcissist is looking at diamond jewellery. Without intervention on your part, they'll have a new diamond watch and Junior will be sleeping in your sister's hand-me-down crib that may or may not have been recalled. Before that happens, take control of the family budget and make sure that the money gets spent on the family's needs.

Accept that you are on your own.

Your narcissist is far more connected with themselves and their own needs than they ever will, or could, be to you and your needs. It's the way their brain works and there is nothing you can do about it. They were like that when you met and had been since childhood.

You can blame them for their behaviour, you can even blame their parents for unleashing such a damaged individual in the world. In many ways, you would be right to do so, but the person you cannot blame for this is yourself.

Instead, accept that you are on your own, do things that make you happy, and practice self-care over your physical, mental and emotional health.

Don't take it personally.

The more you push for your own rights and well-being, the more you protest the actions, words, and attitudes of your narcissist, the more they fail at things, the angrier they will get. They will blame you and anyone else for their troubles, never once looking inward. You have to remember that this is the sort of tantrum you would expect from a spoiled toddler and you need to take it as such and dismiss the blame and insulting language.

Chapter 6:

What is the quickest way to get out of a narcissistic relationship

6.1 Ask for help

You are not alone, and many people have experienced or are experiencing what you are going through. Don't be afraid to ask for help and find a support system to offer you what you need to stay balanced, secure, and self-confident in your choices and journey forward.

It has never been your fault that the person you are in a relationship with doesn't understand their disorder or issue, and even if you were capable of enabling it for a long period of time, you are certainly capable of healing from it and learning how not to repeat the same patterns over and over again.

Help is always available and all around you. If you cannot get to a public support group, or feel comfortable talking to friends and family about it, go online and look for more resources. Find an anonymous group to join if you want to protect your identity. Ask other people what it was like for them and how their recovery process is going. You will learn so much by simply reaching out for help and letting it clear your fears that you are somehow at fault for your experience.

All it takes is awareness and courage, as you let go of the narcissistic relationship. Empowering yourself to enjoy your life more through a balanced partnership is what any person deserves, and you are on the right track to getting there. Heal the patterns so that they are broken and cannot be repeated by offering yourself kindness, staying personal with your journey, process your emotions regularly, take the high road, know the red flags of the narcissist, and seek help whenever you feel like you need support.

You are on your way to becoming the confident, happy, and balanced person you always knew you are and could be. Learning to survive the narcissistic relationship may seem hard at first, but you have all of the tools that you need to accept your story and begin the healing journey.

It is wrong to be in a one-sided relationship with someone who cares only about himself. Such a relationship never ends well, and it is better to see a professional who will help you deal with this kind of situation. In most cases, you are powerless in dealing with such people because they are usually over-possessive. They emotionally trap you into staying in the unhealthy relationship because they feel you belong to them. And they always find a way to blame you for whatever is wrong in the relationship.

They are perfect at shifting the blames to the weaker person in the relationship. They play with your emotion and use it against you.

That is why, in most cases, you feel like you are in a prison. You will be emotionally blackmailed into not seeing walking away as an option.

A mental health professional, however, will help you deal with the relationship right. Sometimes, walking away might not be the solution; you can go through a "pro-dependence oriented" treatment that will help you remain in the relationship but in a much healthier way. The concept of the pro-dependence is to consider the advantage of living with people who challenge us, and channelling our focus on how we benefit from them, rather than considering the vices and dreading what suffering might result in enduring such relationship.

We can benefit a whole lot from their strengths.

Also, they can gain from us. In reality,

you can turn the relationship into a give-and-take thing where both of you end up benefiting from each other.

Probably the best way to cope with the aftermath of breaking it off with a narcissist is finding yourself a decent support group. There are lots of internet-based and real-life groups that you can find in order to discover the stories of others who have been through experiences similar to yours.

Finding individuals who have had run-ins with narcissists in their lives can make it easier to understand that you were never the problem and that these people actually exist in the world. The sooner you get to grasp the reality that narcissists are at fault for their own failed relationships, the sooner you can forgive yourself for allowing the abuse to occur.

In the same light, you might also want to find someone who can shed insight on your unique feelings. Therapists who are well-versed with narcissistic abuse can help you understand your emotions and uncover the truths behind the behaviours of your narcissistic abuser. These people can also provide you valuable coping skills and activities that can make the healing process faster and much more satisfying.

6.2 No contact

For the first few days or weeks after you've finally cut the ties, you might feel the nagging urge to come crawling back and say you're sorry. In typical victim fashion, you might feel like you've done something immensely wrong, leading you to think that you need to offer an apology for acting the way you did.

At this point, you need to remind yourself why you left in the first place. Remind yourself of the abuse and put things into perspective. Recall the pain, the abandonment, the criticism, and the devaluation and realize that these were all real experiences that weren't pleasant for you at all.

Avoid blaming yourself and avoid contact with your abuser at all costs. Give yourself the time to heal and to see things through clear, untainted glasses instead of the blinds that the narc placed over your eyes. If you must, consider taking a break from social media and keeping your phone away from you for the time being. Preoccupy yourself with a hobby and keep your mind busy so you don't end up thinking about your narcissistic abuser.

6.3 Is it always right to leave a narcissist?

Rejecting a narcissist, whether in reality or in their perception, is likely to make them feel incredibly hurt or angry- as it causes a deep narcissistic injury.

A jilted lover may feel a great deal of pain when the source of their affection no longer wants them. So, too, a narcissist feels deeply aggrieved when a source of narcissistic supply- or anyone else for that matter- decides that they are not "good enough."

Extreme narcissists – ever hypervigilant- may feel rejected for reasons that more average people would not. Being too busy or not having a good enough reason to deny their request for your company or collaboration can easily be taken to heart and result in an unexpectedly intense response.

It's best to give them a legitimate reason that is beyond your control than to show that you're choosing to reject them. Being too busy to meet or see them is best if your reason is irrefutable, like having to work late to meet a specific deadline, attend an important wedding, or are booked onto a vacation or trip elsewhere.

Narcissists do not like losing

They really don't. When you say that your relationship is finished, you mean it but the narcissist you are talking to sees that as you throwing down a gauntlet, an invitation to kick into high narcissistic mode and see it as a real challenge and that leads you to:

Narcissists Pursue Victory

He or she won't be chasing after you although that's what it will look like. No, instead they are looking to put things back to how they should be, with them in full control and you bowing down and taking the abuse, while smothering them in adoration and praise.

Believe me when I say this, if you give in and do go back, there will be some form of punishment for the abandonment. He or she does want you back but only on their terms and with the same, if not a higher, degree of selfishness and narcissistic behaviour that was there when you left – why you left.

Narcissists want to keep a constant check on you

Because he or she still loves you? Not likely. Let's face it; they probably never really loved you in the true sense. All he or she wants to do is make sure that you are suffering, that you are not happy and never will be without them in your life. To a narcissist, it is the knowledge that you are truly miserable and suffering without him or her is as satisfying as getting you to go back to them.

At the end of the day, if he or she cannot keep your attention on him or her throughout the relationship then they will want to know that you are constantly thinking of them and really struggling after you are apart. At some point, he or she will offer to end the suffering by accepting your apology and taking you back.

Big mistake – once you are back under their control the abuse will begin again and it will never stop. The most satisfying thing to a narcissist is having you swaying between being with him or her and leaving – that gives the control over you, the ultimate prize for a narcissist.

How to Leave

As long as you are still under the spell of a narcissist, you will be unable to move ahead successfully. This is why it is vital that you leave the person before you can make headway in everything that you do.

However, since you have been in the relationship for a long time, and maybe you two have kids together, you will find it hard to leave the partner.

However, with the right tips, you can leave the person successfully.

Here are the various tips to help you get away from an abusive relationship safely.

Don't Give Them the Last Chance

When you leave an abusive narcissist, they will try to seduce you so that you come back to them and then they will dump you. The main aim of a narcissist is to make sure you are the one to blame in everything.

They want everything to be on their terms, and when it isn't, they find a way to turn the tables around. If the narcissist isn't ready to leave yet, they will turn on the works and plead with you, begging you and telling you how sorry they are.

For you to leave, try and avoid giving them a chance to have the power over you again. They will turn on the begging and then they will plead with you so much, saying how sorry they are and beg you to come back.

Don't Let Them Know You Are Leaving

You don't need to tell the narcissist that you are leaving the relationship. This is because it might make them ready to start love bombing you to trap you in the relationship. They can even threaten to kill themselves just to make you stay on, and they trap you.

Have Some Spare Cash

When you think of leaving, you need to make sure you have some spare cash to get you started with the new life.

Start saving some money early in advance so that when the time comes you leave, you don't have to come back to the person because of the support that they give you. If your partner is an abuser, then you need to do everything in secret so that the person doesn't cut you off entirely.

Report the Abuse

You might not be in the right position to take the situation to the police, but it is vital that you report the abuse. When you go in, make sure you tell what has been happening to you, and you even show the injuries in case you have any that are visible.

When you record a statement, you will have something that you can report when you decide to make a case later on in the future.

Log Out of All Devices

If you stay logged into devices that you shared with your partners, you need to make sure that you change the passwords to devices so that the partner doesn't track you. Make a reset of all the credentials and create new ones.

So, make a list of everything that you have ever signed into, used your credit card on and any autofill, then delete them all.

After logging out of the devices, the next thing is to make sure you aren't being tracked. If possible, dispose of off the phone then get a new one that you can use.

Don't Be Swayed By the Flattery

A narcissist will try and use flattery or any other approach to prevent you from leaving. The goal is to create an environment where you feel that you don't have a choice but to leave.

The narcissist will try to be more than what you ever wanted, and they will do this in various ways, including buying your gifts and giving you the attention you always desired.

Reconnect With Family and Friends

An abusive narcissist will want to cut you away from the family and take up their attention. You might not have been with some of the people that were previously close to you, and you might have neglected them. But the most important thing is for you to reconnect with them so that they assist you in healing.

However, you need to stop feeling shy and embarrassed when they see you. If you have to say sorry, then swallow your pride and apologize.

When you reconnect with them, you will realize how much the people had planned to help you with no success. They might have tried to help, but they didn't know what to do or how to start.

Clean the Decks

This is the right time to identify anyone toxic to your cause and then let them go. You will make a decision, but not everyone will be as understanding as you expect them to be. They will point fingers at you and pretend they are the best in the world.

You need to take this as an opportunity to cut out some people from your life, especially those that are toxic to your goals.

6.4 How to deal with a complicated relationship when children are involved

Dealing with someone who is narcissistic can be tedious, draining, and at times, downright painful, particularly if you are gaining nothing from it. It is even worse when there are children involved. You can begin with seeing if there are any areas that you can change your perspective on. Although you may not like the idea of changing yourself, particularly when the one with narcissism should change, it might be a good place to start.

There are also those who already have children, and do not want to deny them the chance of being raised by both parents. Yet others cite financial reasons; he may be a narcissist, but he's paying the bills. Choosing to stay is a valid choice. You can take control of the relationship and ensure that you do not suffer in the process.

Set boundaries

This is the first step in making sure that your partner does not walk all over you. Make a list of the things that you will not tolerate. This could include name-calling, criticism, threats, yelling, lying, and making demands, and so on.

It is important to write them down as proof. Disrespecting the boundaries should have consequences. If you told your man that the moment he starts shouting, you'll walk away and sleep in the guest bedroom; do just that. He will try to manipulate you to soften your resolve. If you do so, he'll know that he can get away with it.

He'll keep pushing the boundaries, and within no time you'll be right back where you started. Did he change when you decided to set boundaries? You may want to control the way he speaks to you, then he decides not to speak to you at all.

He gives you the silent treatment. This shows that he does not appreciate the boundaries. Don't worry. He doesn't need to.

He only needs to appreciate that they're important for the sake of your relationship. Bring up such conversations when he's in a good mood. He's more likely to listen then.

Listen

People hardly ever listen to narcissists. As soon as they start speaking; people around them are thinking, 'oh, here we go again with the grand talk.' They mentally switch off. And you can hardly blame them. Self-exalting talk is exhausting you know.

Listen to him for a change. He may be praising himself or playing victim yet again, but listen to him anyway. He'll see that you're interested in his welfare, and this will encourage them to treat you better.

Stay Calm

How you behave in times of conflict goes a long way in determining the nature of your relationship with a narcissist.

He will try to provoke you into a reaction so that he can convince himself that he has control over your emotions. Your ability to stay calm robs him of that power. If things seem to be getting out of hand, you can seek help together. Hearing the effect of his behaviour from a neutral party might provoke him to do some soul searching and eventually take steps towards changing.

Conclusion

Narcissism exists on a scale of self-enhancement, with too little, healthy levels, and extreme levels. Unhealthy or extreme narcissism increases as dependence on narcissistic supply increases. Individuals with extreme or unhealthy traits may have underlying self-esteem issues which promote the appeal of narcissistic supply, helping to propagate the addiction, although this is not always the case.

Using the addiction model, we see that people who are dependent on narcissistic supply are "gripped" by narcissism and may act in ways that are extremely detrimental- even abusive- to those around them to maintain the one-directional flow of approval to keep themselves inflated. Rather than fighting to remain in control of narcissism, the narcissist must take responsibility for starving it – perhaps going cold turkey, as an alcoholic or drug addict may choose to do. A narcissist must accept that being ordinary is acceptable and relinquish the drive to stand out as superior from the rest of humanity.

In the long-run, narcissists are unhappy, and make those around them unhappy, meaning that the best option when dealing with a narcissist who is not undergoing a period of self-enlightenment or change (which is highly unlikely in this group), is to cut off or limit contact, depending on the nature of your relationship. As some narcissists are vulnerable to varying self-esteem, and hypervigilant to the slightest insult or threat they may be very sensitive to narcissistic injury. In these cases, the narcissist may become abusive to a degree that even a distant relationship is not possible.

If cutting contact from a narcissist is not possible, other techniques may be employed to make life easier, and avoid infuriating or upsetting them. Avoiding being in their inner circle, whilst remaining warm and approving allows a safe distance to be maintained- making attack or upset far less likely. Causing unnecessary injury to their ego through exposing them as abusive or less than they think themselves to be, rejecting them or outshining them is likely to backfire and cause a great deal of commotion. If peace is the main objective, understanding and avoiding these triggers is preferable.

Making sure that a narcissist delivers on what they may tempt you with, rather than expecting fairness and extending credit, is particularly important when negotiating. Narcissists want to look good and understanding this is the key to channeling them in the right direction, without flooding them with narcissistic supply.

Caution is needed when deciphering what type of narcissistic supply is desired by a narcissist. Flooding them with this or any other attention that makes them feel overly special is likely to further their addiction, as well as draw you into their dangerous inner circle. Remember that you are dealing with a complicated human being, with their own battles to fight, just as you have yours. As dramatic as it sounds, offering up a great deal of narcissistic supply to someone whose well-being is dependent on it may in fact be as morally questionable as supplying an alcoholic or drug addict with a narcotic. Be balanced and fair, without flooding them, when you are able.

Finally, and most importantly, it is our ultimate responsibility to ensure that a narcissist is not able to damage us or our dependents, and that in withdrawing or protecting ourselves we do not damage the narcissist- if possible. The "securing your own oxygen mask" before helping to secure another's scenario on a plane is a good analogy for where our responsibilities should lie- despite narcissists attempts to make you take care of their needs before your own. Leaving an abusive situation should be considered to have the utmost urgency.

However, handling a sensitive or

manipulative person who is non-abusive, should be done so through the lens of someone who can see the humanity of the people involved. Whilst you do not need to have undue sympathy or empathy for a damaging individual, this does not give you free reign to behave badly in return. Your priority is to manage the situation for the good of yourself and your dependents first, but also for everyone that is involved. If the situation cannot be managed well, it may be best to walk away and disengage.

If you have narcissists around you, or if you have been in a relationship with such, you now know why they behave the way they do.
If you were hoping for information on how to change them, you could be a little disappointed. Narcissists hardly ever own up to their problem and consequently refuse to get help.
Those around them are left to do the adjusting. Having read this book, you can now deal much better with them.

If you're in a relationship with a narcissist, you don't necessarily have to leave, although that becomes the only option in worst-case scenarios. You can choose to stay and take control. You can establish healthy boundaries that your partner must abide with.

If you've already been through a relationship and have come out with scars, we included the information on healing from emotional abuse just for you. You do not have to allow that experience to scar you for life. You can pick up the pieces.

Begin by accepting what happened. Leaving in denial will only hold you back from recovery. Are you dealing with stress, anxiety, panic attacks or depression as a result? You know the source of the problem, and that is what you have to deal with. You cannot change the one who hurt you, but you can change yourself. You can lift that self-esteem that was shredded by the abuse. Practice positive affirmations. Say good things about yourself, and with the time you'll begin to live your words.

Thank you for reaching the end of this book. I hope it was of great help to you.

Made in the USA
Middletown, DE
05 June 2020